WELCOME TO CANADIAN ENGLISH

A BASIC HANDBOOK FOR STUDENTS LIVING IN ONTARIO PART 2

AUTHORS: LILLIAN BUTOVSKY / ESTHER PODOLIAK

The Ontario Ministry of Citizenship and Culture

Susan Fish, Minister

Credits

Assistance with editing, writing and co-ordinating: John McHugh
Illustrations: Ken Gray, Advertising
Design: H. Bruce Dorland & Assoc.
Photography: Unexpected Company and Simon Glass

Drug label samples on pages 174 and 175 copyrighted by Pharmex, U.S.A. and distributed in Canada by Pharmasystems, Inc.

Works of art in photo stories:

On page 263, in photo no. 16:
Alfred Joseph Casson, 1898-
White Pine, c. 1957
oil on canvas
The McMichael Canadian Collection
Anonymous Donor

On page 264, in photo no. 17:
Roy Harvey Thomas, 1949- (Ojibwa)
Thunderbird and Young, 1975
acrylic on canvas
The McMichael Canadian Collection
Purchase 1975

On page 264, in photo no. 18:
Peter Angutik, 1934- (Povungnituk)
Woman Nursing Child
soapstone
The McMichael Canadian Collection
Purchase 1968

Published by the
Ministry of Citizenship and Culture.
Printed by the Queen's Printer
for Ontario
Province of Ontario
Toronto, Canada

© 1985 Government of Ontario

Copies available at $2.00 from the
Ontario Government Bookstore,
880 Bay St., Toronto
for personal shopping.
Out-of-town customers write to
Publications Services Section,
5th Floor, 880 Bay St., Toronto, Ontario,
M7A 1N8. Telephone 965-6015.
Toll free long distance 1-800-268-7540;
in Northwestern Ontario 0-Zenith 67200.

D1476 2/85 15M
ISBN-0-7743-9975-9

CONTENTS

Part 2 of "Welcome to Canadian English" is a continuation of Part 1. Here are the main characters (They all appeared in Part 1 except David):

Ana Pinto: a recent immigrant from Chile
Tony Faria: a recent immigrant from Portugal
Lou Wong: from China, now a Canadian citizen
Su Ping Wong: also Chinese, and Lou's wife
Ken and David Wong: sons of Lou and Su Ping

Here is a brief summary of Part 1:

Tony and Ana met for the first time in an English class. One day they walked out of class together. They were both going to King Street. Ana was going home. Tony was going to his job as a painter's assistant; he was painting a house on King Street at that time.

Ana also met Lou, because Lou is Tony's employer. One day, while Ana was walking along King Street, she ran into Lou and Tony painting. Tony introduced Lou to Ana.

One evening, Lou's younger son, Ken, tripped over some roller skates on the stairs and hurt himself. Lou called an ambulance and took Ken to the hospital. They bandaged up Ken's arm. Later Lou made a follow-up appointment for Ken with the doctor.

Tony and Lou got to know one another on the job. They ate lunch together and Lou helped Tony with his English. They talked about their former occupations. Lou was a painter in China, but Tony wasn't a painter in Portugal. He was a musician; he played piano and clarinet.

Here are some other events in Part 1: Su Ping and Lou went grocery shopping together; Su Ping went shopping for shoes and took Ken along; and Ana went to the post office to mail a package to Chile.

SPEAKING ACTIVITY

Are there any students in your class who studied Part 1? Ask them questions about the characters or events in Part 1. If they don't have the answers, perhaps you will find some of the answers in Part 2.

UNIT 16: YOUR FIRST JOB

VOCABULARY: For the Conversation کفتگو - مذاکره

Nouns
1. factory
2. work or a job

Verb
3. (to) worry

Adjectives
4. nervous
5. fine

BEFORE THE CONVERSATION: Ana Gets a Job

Ana didn't work in Chile. She was a student.

Last week she went to a factory for a job.

She got the job.

She started work yesterday.

CONVERSATION: Ana's First Job

First, look at ALL the pictures. Then look at EACH picture.
WHAT IS THE PERSON SAYING? TRY TO GUESS.

Words for the Conversation on page 136.

EXTENSION WITH CHOICES

Make three conversations.

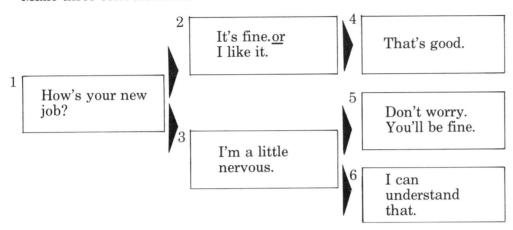

1. How's your new job?

2. It's fine. or I like it.

3. I'm a little nervous.

4. That's good.

5. Don't worry. You'll be fine.

6. I can understand that.

COMMUNICATION ACTIVITY

Part I
Take a partner. You are A. Your partner is B.

A

Ask questions like these.

1. a. What was your first job?
   b. How was it?
2. a. Do you remember your first date?
   b. How did you feel?
3. a. Where was your first English class?
   b. How was it?

B

Answer the questions.
Here are some answers for the **b** questions.

4. It was fine.
5. I felt fine.
6. I liked it.
7. I was a little nervous.
8. I was very nervous.
9. I never want to go through that again.

PART II
Ask some people in your class about a first experience, job, date or English class.
Write the person's name and check off "Liked it" or "Didn't like it."
If the person didn't like it, ask why and write the reason.

NAME	EXPERIENCE	LIKED IT	DIDN'T LIKE IT	REASON
Ana	first job		✓	She was nervous.

Continue in your notebook.

WORDS FOR THE CONVERSATION

1. I got a job.
2. Oh. Good.
3. Where?
4. In a factory.
5. What are your hours?
6. Seven-thirty to four.
7. I'm a little nervous. It's my first job.
8. Don't worry.
9. You'll be fine.

Other Sentences You May Hear

Picture 5: What hours are you working?
What hours will you be working?
Picture 9: You'll be all right.
You'll be okay.

COMMUNICATION ACTIVITY: How You Feel

You want to know how to say how you feel. Mime each picture, and say to the teacher:

How do you say this? <u>and</u> Please spell it. <u>or</u>
How do you spell it?

Write the word under each picture.

1 worried. 2 3 4 5
6 7 8 9

The answers are on page 270.

READING AND WRITING: Job Application Form

When Ana applied for a job, she filled out a form.
This is one page of the form.

APPLICATION FORM

Please Print

PERSONAL		
1	Surname **Pinto**	First **Ana**	Middle **Sara**

2	Address **21 King St.**	Apt. No.	City **Toronto**

3	Province **Ontario**	Postal Code **M4P 3K3**	Home Phone	A/C **416** — Number **211 3663**

4 | Are you legally entitled to work in Canada? Yes ☑ No ☐
(Those so entitled are Canadian Citizens, Landed Immigrants or holders of valid work permits)
Are you of legal working age? Yes ☑ No ☐

EDUCATION

5	Schools Attended	Nature of Education	Level Achieved
Academic	Liceo Número Siete	Secondary School	High School Graduation Diploma
Vocational			
Professional			

6	Scholastic Honours, Scholarships, etc.	Patents obtained, papers or books published:

7	Seminars, Training, etc.	What special technical skills do you have?

8 | Evening Extension / Correspondence Courses:
I am studying English at Bond St. School, evenings.

9 | Have you completed an Apprenticeship? Yes ☐ No ☑ If yes, please describe.

10 | Are you a licensed Journeyman? Yes ☐ No ☑ If yes, please describe.

11 | Are you willing to relocate? Yes ☑ No ☐
Is there a geographical location to which you are not willing to relocate? Yes ☑ No ☐ If yes, please specify.
I would like to be near Toronto

12 | Have you a valid Operator's license? Yes ☐ No ☑
Have you a valid Chauffeur's license? Yes ☐ No ☑   If necessary for the job, could you have a car at your disposal? Yes ☐ No ☑

13 | If necessary for the job, would you be willing to make a bonding application? Yes ☑ No ☐

14	Position Desired **light assembly**	Salary/Wage Expected $ **5-6.00** per annum ☐ per hour ☑	Availability Yr/Mo/Day **now**

137

Fill this out with information about yourself.

APPLICATION FORM

Please Print

PERSONAL		
1 **Surname**	**First**	**Middle**
2 **Address**	**Apt. No.** / **City**	
3 **Province**	**Postal Code**	**Home Phone** — A/C Number

4 Are you legally entitled to work in Canada?   Yes ☐   No ☐
(Those so entitled are Canadian Citizens, Landed Immigrants or holders of valid work permits)
Are you of legal working age?   Yes ☐   No ☐

EDUCATION		
5 Schools Attended	Nature of Education	Level Achieved
Academic		
Vocational		
Professional		

6 Scholastic Honours, Scholarships, etc.	Patents obtained, papers or books published:
7 Seminars, Training, etc.	What special technical skills do you have?

8 Evening Extension / Correspondence Courses:

9 Have you completed an Apprenticeship?   Yes ☐   No ☐   If yes, please describe.

10 Are you a licensed Journeyman?   Yes ☐   No ☐   If yes, please describe.

11 Are you willing to relocate?   Yes ☐   No ☐
Is there a geographical location to which you are not willing to relocate?   Yes ☐   No ☐   If yes, please specify.

12 Have you a valid Operator's license?   Yes ☐   No ☐   If necessary for the job, could you have a car at your disposal?   Yes ☐   No ☐
Have you a valid Chauffeur's license?   Yes ☐   No ☐

13 If necessary for the job, would you be willing to make a bonding application?   Yes ☐   No ☐

14 Position Desired	Salary/Wage Expected	Availability
	$ _____ per annum ☐ per hour ☐	Yr/Mo/Day

USEFUL INFORMATION: Job Application Form

1. A job application form has many questions.

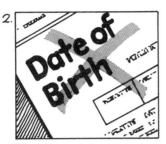

2. The form cannot ask your age or birthdate.

3. The form can ask if you are between the ages of 18 and 65.

4. There is a law* about this.

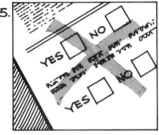

5. It tells which questions cannot be asked

6. and which questions can be asked.

7. If you find a question that is not lawful

8. you don't have to write the answer.

Some of the questions below are <u>lawful</u>. قانونی
They are on the application form on page 138.
Some of the questions below are not lawful.
They are not on the application form.
Look at each question below.
Is it on the application form?
Write **Yes** or **No** beside each question.

Is this a legal question?

9. Are you legally entitled to work in Canada?		Yes
10. Are you a Canadian citizen or a landed immigrant?		No
11. What level of education did you achieve?		_____
12. What special honours or scholarships did you achieve?		_____
13. What's your country of origin?		_____
14. What's the name and location of the elementary school you attended?		_____
15. What's your religion?		_____
16. What's your sex, male or female? Sex جنس		_____
17. Do you have any physical handicaps?		_____

*This law is part of the Ontario Human Rights Code.
If you have a question, call the Ontario Human Rights Commission.
You can also ask for a book entitled "Employment Application Forms and Interviews."

GRAMMAR: More About the Verb Be

1

I'm a little nervous.

Am is a form of the verb **be**.

Short form: I'm a little nervous.
Long form: I am a little nervous.

2. Here is the verb **be** with the
pronouns **we** and **they**.

a.

We are happy.
We're happy.

b.

They are my friends.
They're my friends.

3. Here is the verb **be** with
nouns.

c.

The boy is tired.
The boy's tired.

d.

The boys are tired.

3. Make sentences with the verb **be**.

a.

They're painters.

e.

_____ _____

b.

She's my friend.

f.

_____ _____

c.

_____ _____

g.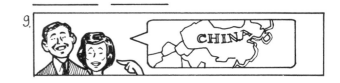

_____ _____

d.

_____ _____ _____

h.

_____ _____

The answers are on page 270.

PRONUNCIATION: Singular vs. Plural

1. **The boy is tired** is often <u>pronounced</u> **The boy's tired.**
2. Sometimes it is <u>difficult</u> to hear the <u>difference</u> between sentences like these:

   a. Singular: The boy's tired.
   b. Plural: The boys are tired.

3. Listen to each sentence that the teacher says.

   If you hear a singular noun, draw one <u>body</u>.
   If you hear a plural noun, draw two bodies.

a.

singular

b.

plural

4. _____ 5. _____ 6. _____ 7. _____ 8. _____ 9. _____ 10. _____ 11. _____ 12. _____

EXTRA STUDY: Crossword Puzzle

Look in the dictionary, if necessary.
Across
  2. This means "work."
  5. The verb is "worry."
     The adjective is ___.
  7. This means "not well."
  8. Short form for "etcetera."
 12. After the first.
 13. Opposite of "cold."
 14. This is how you feel if you don't sleep or if you work many hours.
 16. A clock tells you the ___.
 17. Opposite of "subtract."
Down
  1. Opposite of "hot."
  3. A job.
  4. Opposite of "sick."
  6. Ana is nervous because this is her ___ job.
  9. You need this item of clothing when the weather is cold.
 10. This word can mean "upset."
 11. This colour is the opposite of "black."
 15. You need this little word to make a question in the past tense.

The answers are on page 270.

VOCABULARY: For the Conversation

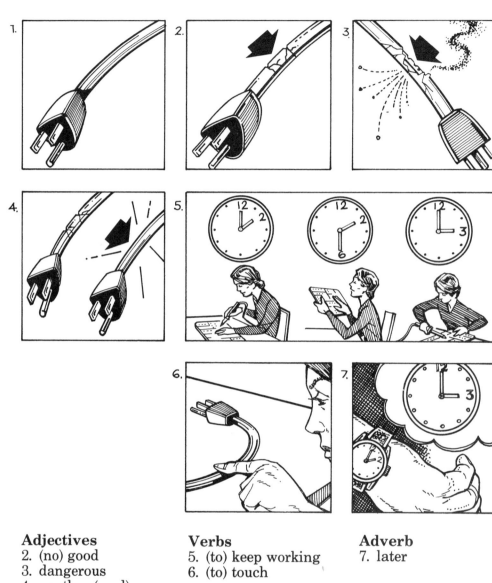

Noun
1. a cord

Adjectives
2. (no) good
3. dangerous
4. another (cord)

Verbs
5. (to) keep working
6. (to) touch

Adverb
7. later

CONVERSATION: Ana Insists on Safety

First, look at ALL the pictures. Then look at EACH picture.
WHAT IS THE PERSON SAYING? TRY TO GUESS.

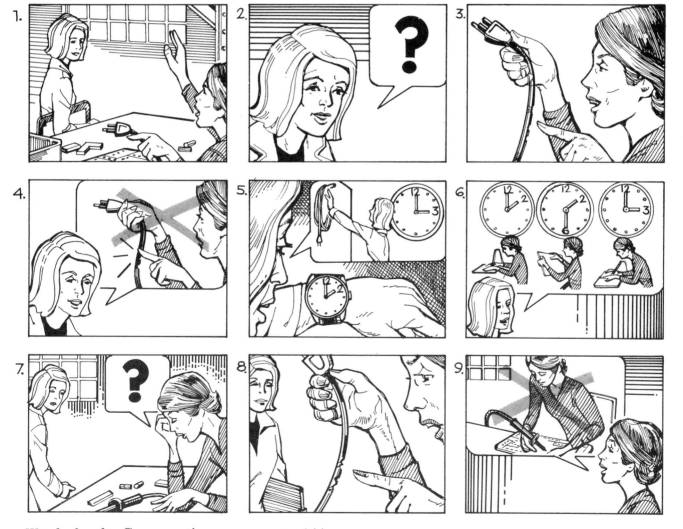

Words for the Conversation are on page 144.

EXTENSION WITH CHOICES

Make two conversations.

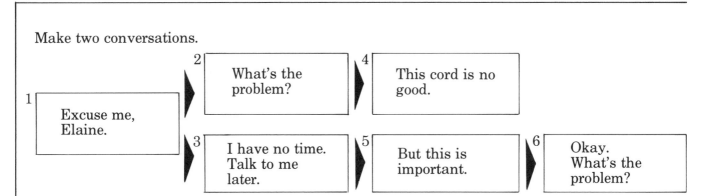

SPEAKING ACTIVITY

Take a partner. One of you is A. The other one is B.

A 😊   B 😊   A 😊

Get B's attention.
You can say:

Tell A that you can't talk now.
Give an excuse.
You can say:

Be persistent.
Make sure that B talks to you now or later.
You can say:

1. Excuse me, Elaine.	2. I have no time. I have to make a phone call. 3. I'm expecting a visitor. 4. It's my lunch hour. 5. I'm expecting a ___. 6. It's my ___.

7. But this is very important.
8. But this is really important.
9. This will only take a minute.
10. Can I see you right after that?
11. Can I see you when you're finished.

WORDS FOR THE CONVERSATION

1. Excuse me, Elaine.
2. What's the problem?
3. This <u>cord</u> is no good.
4. Don't touch it.
5. I'll get another one later.
6. Keep working.
7. (to herself) I don't know what to do.
8. It's dangerous.
9. I don't want to use it.

Other Sentences You May Hear

Picture 3: This cord is cracked.
Picture 6: Continue working.
Don't stop working.
Picture 7: What should I do now?
What do I do now?
Picture 8: It's not safe.

READING: Safety Signs

Look at the pictures. Read the signs.

a.

Danger. Work overhead.

b.

Beware of electrical wires.

c.

Know the location of fire extinguishers and exits.

d.

Danger. Keep out.

e.

Protect your hearing.

f.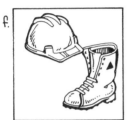

Hard hats and safety boots must be worn on this project.

g.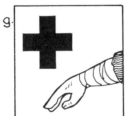

Be sure. Get first aid.

h.

Danger. High voltage.

i.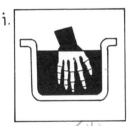

Danger. Corrosive materials.

j.

Eye protection must be worn.

k.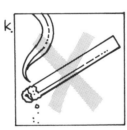

No smoking.

Here are the pictures without the signs. Can you remember the signs?

a.
b.
c.
d.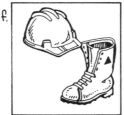

e.
f.
g.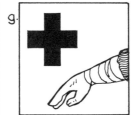
h.

i.
j.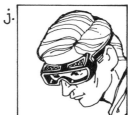
k.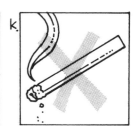

Match the picture to the sign and put the letter in the box.

1 [e] Protect your hearing.

2 [ ] Danger. Work overhead.

3 [ ] Danger. Keep out.

4 [ ] Be sure. Get first aid.

5 [h] Danger. High voltage.

6 [ ] Eye protection must be worn.

7 [ ] Danger. Corrosive materials.

8 [ ] Beware of electrical wires.

9 [ ] Know the location of fire extinguishers and exits.

10 [f] Hard hats and safety boots must be worn on this project.

11 [k] No smoking.

146

USEFUL INFORMATION: The Right to Refuse*

1.
If you are working with something dangerous, tell the supervisor.

2.
If it doesn't get fixed, speak up again.

3.
Your complaint must be investigated

4.
in front of you and a worker's representative.

5.
If the supervisor still doesn't think there is danger,

6.
and you still really believe there is danger to yourself or another worker,

7.
an inspector from the Ministry of Labour must be called.

8.
Wait in a safe place near your work (unless you are given other work)

9.
until the inspector's investigation is complete.

10.
Under Ontario Law** you can't be fired for refusing to work in unsafe conditions.

11.
If your employer has fired you or penalized you,

12.
and you think it is for this reason, you can ask for help.***

*The Occupational Health and Safety Act, section 23. Call the Ontario Ministry of Labour for information in different languages.
**The same act, section 24.
***Call your union if you have one, or the Ontario Labour Relations Board.

GRAMMAR I: Making Offers with Will

I'll get another cord.

Elaine is offering to get another cord.
The word **will** is used to show an offer.
It comes before the base form of the verb.
The base form is the infinitive without **to**.

Short form: I'll get another cord.

Long form: I will get another cord.

2. Here are more examples of offers with **will**.

a.
My stomach hurts. I'll call the doctor.

b.
This pencil is no good. I'll get another pencil.

3. Make offers. Use the verbs **get** and **call**.

a.

I'll get another cord.

e.

— — — — —

b.

— — — — —

f.

— — — — —

c.

— — — — —

g.

— — — — —

d.

— — — — —

h.

— — — — —

The answers are on page 270.

GRAMMAR II: Want   Before a Verb.

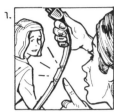

1.

I don't want
to use it.

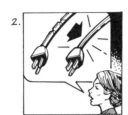

2.

I want to have
another cord.

3 After **want** or **wants** we use the infinitive form of the verb.

I You We They My friends	don't want want	to walk to work. to take the bus. to work on Saturday. to get a job.
He She Ana My friend	doesn't want wants	to eat lunch now. to live in Ottawa. to play the piano.

4. Make sentences. Use **want** or **wants**.   Make sentences. Use **don't want** or **doesn't want**.

a.

I want to work.

e.

She doesn't want to live in Ottawa.

b.

f.

c.

g.

d.

h.

_ _ _ _ _ _ _ _ _   _ _ _ _ _ _ _ _ _

The answers are on page 270.

5. Make sentences about yourself and someone you know.

I want to _____.   I don't want to _____.

My (friend) wants to _____.   My (friend) doesn't want to _____.

UNIT 18: MAKING COMPLAINTS

VOCABULARY: For the Conversation

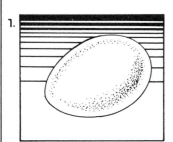
1.

2.

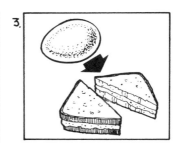
3.

4.

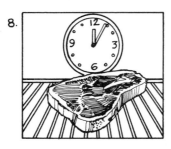
5.

6.

7.

8.

9.

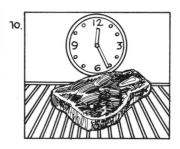
10.

11.

12.

Nouns
1. an egg
2. a sandwich
3. an egg sandwich
4. a salad
5. a Greek salad
6. spaghetti
7. a steak

Adjectives
8. rare
9. medium
10. well done

Verbs
11. (to) order
12. (to) get

CONVERSATION: Lou's Family in the Restaurant

First, look at ALL the pictures. Then look at EACH picture.
WHAT IS THE PERSON SAYING? TRY TO GUESS.

Words for the Conversation on page 157.

EXTENSION WITH CHOICES

Make as many conversations as you can.

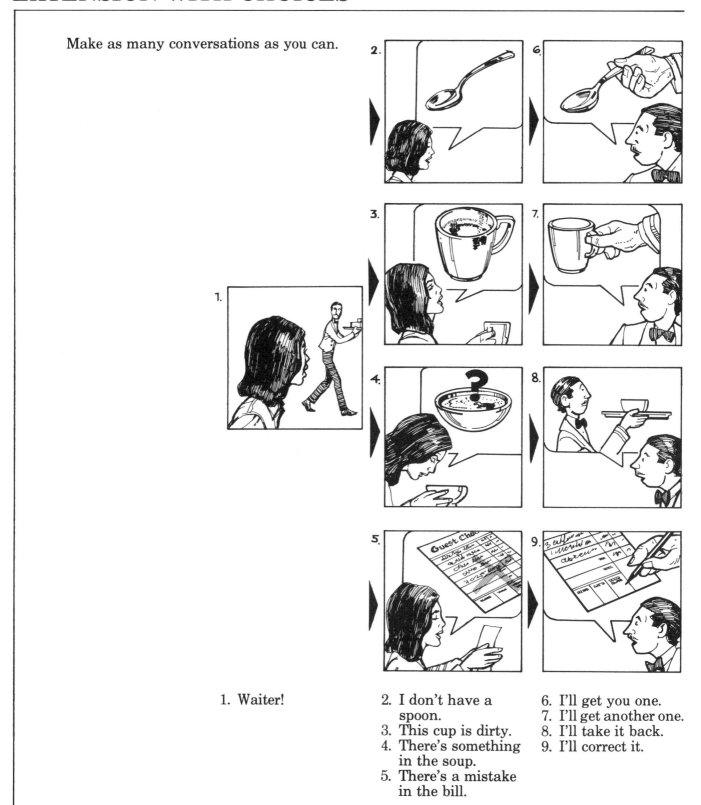

1. Waiter!

2. I don't have a spoon.
3. This cup is dirty.
4. There's something in the soup.
5. There's a mistake in the bill.

6. I'll get you one.
7. I'll get another one.
8. I'll take it back.
9. I'll correct it.

GRAMMAR: Negative Statements in the Past

 I didn't order this.

 I ordered a salad.

3. To make a negative statement in the past, put **didn't** before the base form of the verb.

4. Here are more examples:

We didn't watch television last night.   She didn't work in 1982.
They didn't live in Chile in 1980.   Ana didn't live in Canada in 1979.

5. Last night Tony had a lazy night. Make sentences. Use **didn't**.

a.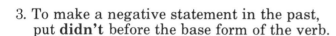

He didn't work.

e.

b.

f.

c.

g.

d.

h.

The answers are on page 270.

6. Tell about yourself.

Last night I didn't _____ .

VOCABULARY: From the Menu

Verbs
1. (to) fry
2. (to) grill
3. (to) bake
4. (to) roast
5. (to) chop
6. (to) mash

Nouns
7. tomato juice
8. shrimp cocktail
9. hamburger on a bun
10. cottage cheese
11. fish
12. liver
13. mushrooms
14. bacon
15. (french fried) potatoes
16. spinach
17. chef salad
18. (fried) onion rings
19. cole slaw
20. ice cream cone
21. ice cream
22. pie
23. blueberries
24. apples
25. jello with whipped cream

READING: Restaurant Menu

Menu

APPETIZERS

tomato juice _____ .45
soup du jour _____ .80
shrimp cocktail _3.50

BURGERS

hamburger_____ 1.50
hamburger with cottage
cheese, no bun _____ 2.50

ENTRÉES

	DINNER...includes soup or juice and beverage.	A LA CARTE
1. Spaghetti with tomato sauce	4.95	3.95
with meat sauce	5.15	4.15
2. Grilled sirloin steak	7.75	6.75
3. Baked fish	6.95	5.95
4. Baby beef liver with bacon or onions	5.25	4.25
5. Chopped steak with mushroom sauce	6.25	5.25
6. Roast beef	6.75	5.75

All entrées come with potatoes (baked, mashed or French fried) and vegetables.

COLD PLATES

Cold Roast Beef_ 4.00
Greek Salad_____ 3.75
Spinach Salad___ 2.50
Chef Salad_____ 1.65

SIDE ORDERS

French fries _____ .90
Fried onion rings ___ 1.50
Cole slaw_____ 1.10
Cottage cheese _____ 1.00

DESSERTS

Ice Cream (chocolate,
vanilla, strawberry)_ 1.00
Pie (blueberry, apple)_ 2.00
with ice cream _____ 2.50
with cheese _____ 2.25
Jello with whipped cream_ .80

BEVERAGES

Coffee _____ .45
Sanka _____ .50
Tea _____ .45
Cola _____ .50
Milk _____ .50

PERSONAL: Things You Like/Don't Like on the Menu

1. Look at the menu.

Write the names of three things that you like.

First: _____

Second: _____

Third: _____

2. Look at the menu.

Write the names of three things that you don't like.

First: _____

Second: _____

Third: _____

SPEAKING ACTIVITIES

I. Taking an Order

a. Take a partner.
b. You are the waiter or waitress.
   Your partner's book is open at the menu on page 155.
   Take your partner's order.
c. Write out a bill.
d. Your partner checks the bill to see if it's correct.
e. Then switch.
   Your partner is the waiter or waitress.

Guest Check		
TAX		
TOTAL	$	

CHECK NO.	WAITER	NO. OF GUESTS	

II. Inviting Somebody for Dinner

Take a partner. Invite your partner for dinner. Then ask questions like these:

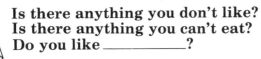

Is there anything you don't like?
Is there anything you can't eat?
Do you like _____?

Write your partner's name and answers in your notebook.

III. Talking About What You Eat

Ask your partner questions like these:

What do you usually eat for lunch?
What's in it?
How do you prepare it?

Write your partner's name and answers in your notebook.

WORDS FOR THE CONVERSATION

1. Are you ready to order now?
2. Yes. He'll have an egg sandwich.
3. He'll have spaghetti.
4. I'll have Greek salad.
5. I'll have a steak, medium rare.
6. I didn't order this.
7. I ordered a salad.
8. I'm sorry.
9. I'll get the salad right away.

Other Sentences You May Hear

Picture 1: Would you like to order now?
Picture 2: Yes. He'd like an egg sandwich.
Picture 3: He'd like spaghetti.
Picture 4: I'd like a Greek salad.

Picture 5: I'd like a steak, medium rare.
Picture 6: This isn't what I ordered.
Picture 9: I'll bring the salad right away.

EXTRA STUDY: Crossword Puzzle

Down
1. You can start your meal with this food.
3. Opposite of "clean."
4. You ___ food in a restaurant from the waiter.
5. This (female) person takes your order in the restaurant.
6. This is what you pay in the restaurant after you eat.
8. Another word for Number 6 above.

Across
2. Opposite of "come."
5. This (male) person takes your order in a restaurant.
6. You can drink coffee in this.
7. An error.
9. You need this to cut your food.
10. You can drink water out of this.

The answers are on page 270.

157

UNIT 19: CALLING IN TO REPORT ABSENCE

CONVERSATION: Ana Calls In Sick

First, look at ALL the pictures. Then look at EACH picture.
WHAT IS THE PERSON SAYING? TRY TO GUESS.

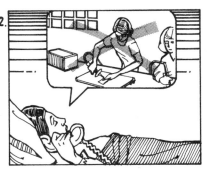

Words for the Conversation on page 161.

READING: Handwritten Telephone Messages

Ana called the factory. Here is the message that the receptionist gave Elaine.

> Elaine—
> Ana called. She can't come to work today. She's sick.

Sometimes handwritten messages are difficult to read. Here are more messages. What does each one say? Circle the number of the correct answer.

A.

> Tony—
> Lou called. Please go to 351 Queen St. in the morning.

1. Please go to 351 Main St.
2. Please go to 351 Queen St.
3. Please go to 351 Green St.

B.

> Tony—
> Ana called. Don't worry. The new job was fine.

1. The new job was fine.
2. The new job was fun.

C.

> Elaine—
> Ana called. She'll be back at work Tuesday.

1. She'll be back at work Thursday.
2. He'll be back at work Tuesday.
3. She'll be back at work Tuesday.

D.

> Lou—
> Your wife called. Please call as soon as you can.

1. Please come as soon as you can.
2. Please call as soon as you can.
3. Please call as soon as you come.

E.

> Tony—
> Ana called. Her friend is arriving from Chile tonight.

1. Her friend is arriving from Chile today.
2. Her friend is arriving from China tonight.
3. Her friend is arriving from Chile tonight.

F.

> Sylvia—
> Ana called. She doesn't know where the wedding is.

1. Ana doesn't know when the wedding is.
2. Ana doesn't know where the wedding is.
3. Ada doesn't know when the wedding is.

The answers are on page 270.

EXPRESSIONS OF TIME: Future and Past

I. Expressions of Future Time
Today is September 10. You are home sick. When will you be back at work?

tomorrow

the day
after tomorrow

on Thursday

next Monday or
next week or
in a week

in two weeks or
two weeks from
today

II. Expressions of Past Time
Today is September 20. You are at work now. You were home sick.
When were you home sick?

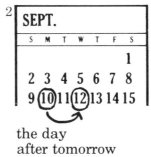

yesterday

the day before
yesterday or
two days ago

on Monday

last Friday

two weeks ago

160

III. Listening

Listen to today's date. Write it in your notebook. Listen to the time expression.
Write the second date in your notebook.

JAN.	FEB.	MAR.
S M T W T F S	S M T W T F S	S M T W T F S
1 2 3 4 5 6 7	1 2 3 4	1 2 3
8 9 10 11 12 13 14	5 6 7 8 9 10 11	4 5 6 7 8 9 10
15 16 17 18 19 20 21	12 13 14 15 16 17 18	11 12 13 14 15 16 17
22 23 24 25 26 27 28	19 20 21 22 23 24 25	18 19 20 21 22 23 24
29 30 31	26 27 28 29	25 26 27 28 29 30 31

APRIL	MAY	JUNE
S M T W T F S	S M T W T F S	S M T W T F S
1 2 3 4 5 6 7	1 2 3 4 5	1 2
8 9 10 11 12 13 14	6 7 8 9 10 11 12	3 4 5 6 7 8 9
15 16 17 18 19 20 21	13 14 15 16 17 18 19	10 11 12 13 14 15 16
22 23 24 25 26 27 28	20 21 22 23 24 25 26	17 18 19 20 21 22 23
29 30	27 28 29 30 31	24 25 26 27 28 29 30

JULY	AUG.	SEPT.
S M T W T F S	S M T W T F S	S M T W T F S
1 2 3 4 5 6 7	1 2 3 4	1
8 9 10 11 12 13 14	5 6 7 8 9 10 11	2 3 4 5 6 7 8
15 16 17 18 19 20 21	12 13 14 15 16 17 18	9 10 11 12 13 14 15
22 23 24 25 26 27 28	19 20 21 22 23 24 25	16 17 18 19 20 21 22
29 30 31	26 27 28 29 30 31	23 30 24 25 26 27 28 29

OCT.	NOV.	DEC.
S M T W T F S	S M T W T F S	S M T W T F S
1 2 3 4 5 6	1 2 3	1
7 8 9 10 11 12 13	4 5 6 7 8 9 10	2 3 4 5 6 7 8
14 15 16 17 18 19 20	11 12 13 14 15 16 17	9 10 11 12 13 14 15
21 22 23 24 25 26 27	18 19 20 21 22 23 24	16 17 18 19 20 21 22
28 29 30 31	25 26 27 28 29 30	23 30 24 31 25 26 27 28 29

Look at each circled date. Write the time expression in your notebook.

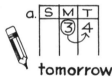
a. tomorrow

b.

c.

d.

e.

f.

WORDS FOR THE CONVERSATION

1. This is Ana Pinto.
2. I can't come to work today.
3. I'm sick.
4. How do you spell your name?
5. P-I-N-T-O.
6. When will you be back at work?
7. Tomorrow, I hope.
8. Who's your supervisor?
9. Elaine.
10. Okay. I'll tell her.
11. Thank you.
12. Goodbye.

Other Sentences You May Hear

Picture 1: This is Ana Pinto speaking.
Picture 2: I won't be able to come to work today.
Picture 6: Do you know when you'll be back?
Picture 8: What's your supervisor's name?
Picture 10: Okay. I'll give her the message.

GRAMMAR AND PRONUNCIATION: Can and Can't

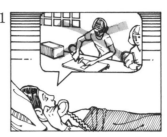

1

2

I can't come to work today.

I can come to work tomorrow.

3 The words **can't** and **can** come before the base form of the verb.

I You She/He/Ana We/They My friend My friends	**can't** **can**	visit today. watch television today. work today. work Monday. come to work tomorrow. come to school today.

4. Listen to the rhythm and stress of this sentence. **Can't** is stressed.

¹ ② ③ 4 ⑤ 6 ⑦

I **can't come** to **work** to**day**

5. Listen to the rhythm and stress of this sentence. **Can** gets no stress in a statement. The vowel **a** in **can** is prounounced (ə). Don't put stress on the word **can**; people might think that you are saying **can't**.

¹ 2 ③ 4 ⑤ 6 ⑦

I can **come** to **work** to**day**

6. Listen to the teacher's sentence and respond with "That's good" or "That's too bad," for example:

Teacher: Tony can't come to school today.　　Student: That's too bad.

Teacher: Ana can come for lunch.　　Student: That's good.

7. Make sentences. Use **can't** or **can.**

a.

He can't play the clarinet on Tuesday.

b.

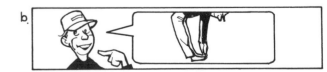

I can touch my toes

The answers are on page 270.

BINGO GAME

9:50 am	A-B-D	fifth	shoe	September
9:50 pm	A-B-B	sixth	shoes	December
4:13	P-A-S	coat	man	I like my job.
4:30	P-A-F	coats	men	I liked my job.
Tuesday	first	watch	woman	The boy's tired.
Thursday	third	watches	women	The boys are tired.

Copy 24 items from above into the 24 places below, in random order. Listen. If you hear an item, check it in pencil. When you have checked a row of items, either vertical, horizontal or diagonal, call out "Bingo."

		■		

USEFUL INFORMATION: Sick Leave

1. Ana was off work, sick.

2. Her employer paid for her sick leave.

3. Some employers pay you when you are sick.

4. Some don't.

5. If you are <u>absent</u> for a <u>certain</u> number of days,

6. some employers ask for a doctor's <u>certificate</u>.

7. If you are working, ask your employer about sick <u>benefits</u>.

8. You can say: "What is the <u>policy</u> on sick leave?"

9. If your employer doesn't pay for your sick leave,

10. you can apply for <u>Unemployment Insurance.</u>*

11. If you get hurt on the job,

12. tell your employer right away.**

*Contact the nearest Canada Employment Centre.
**If you can't work because of an injury, you can apply for Workers' Compensation. The Workers' Compensation Board office is listed in the blue pages of your telephone <u>directory</u>.

164

UNIT 20: DAYCARE FOR YOUR CHILD

VOCABULARY: For the Conversation

1. nursery or daycare centre
2. child
3. teacher
4. supervisor

CONVERSATION: Su Ping Calls A Daycare Centre

First, look at ALL the pictures. Then look at EACH picture.
WHAT IS THE PERSON SAYING? TRY TO GUESS.

Words for the Conversation are on page 169.

USEFUL INFORMATION: Choosing a Daycare Centre

Not all daycare centres are the same.

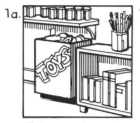

1a. This one is safe.

1b. This one is not.

2a. The teachers watch the children.

2b. The teachers don't watch the children.

3a. The children look happy.

3b. The children don't look happy.

4a. The teachers look friendly.

4b. The teachers don't look friendly.

5a. The children are warm.

5b. The children are cold.

6a. This one is clean.

6b. This one is not.

7a. There's plenty of room.

7b. It's crowded.

8a. This one is inexpensive.

8b. This one is expensive.

COMMUNICATION ACTIVITY: Choosing a Daycare Centre

Take a partner. One of you is A. The other one is B.
You and your partner have a child.
You are choosing a nursery for your child.
A visits the nursery on this page.
B visits the nursery on the next page.

 A

You visit Nursery A. Look at the picture below.

Write four things you like and four things you don't like in Nursery A.

Things I Like

1. _____

2. _____

3. _____

4. _____

Things I Don't Like

1. _____

2. _____

3. _____

4. _____

You visit nursery B. Look at the picture below. B

Write four things you like and four things you don't like in Nursery B.

Things I Like

1. _____

2. _____

3. _____

4. _____

Things I Don't Like

1. _____

2. _____

3. _____

4. _____

A

Describe Nursery A to your partner.
Tell what you like and what you don't like.

B

Describe Nursery B to your partner.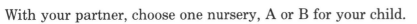
Tell what you like and don't like.

With your partner, choose one nursery, A or B for your child.

WORDS FOR THE CONVERSATION

1. Hello.
2. May I please speak to the supervisor?
3. I'm sorry. She's not here.
4. Can I help you?
5. I'd like to visit the nursery.
6. I'm looking for a place for my child.
7. How old is your child?
8. Three.
9. Can you come Thursday at 9:00?
10. Yes. Thank you.

Other Sentences You May Hear

Picture 2: Is the supervisor there please?
           I'd like to talk to the supervisor please.
Picture 3: I'm sorry. She isn't in.
Picture 8: What age is your child?
Picture 10: Is Thursday at 9:00 okay?

SPEAKING ACTIVITY

Ask some people in your class these questions.

1. Do you have any children?
2. (If yes) how many?
3. What are their names?
4. How old are they?
5. Are any of your children in daycare?
6. What do you like about that daycare?
7. What do you dislike about it?

Write the names of the people and the answers to your questions in your notebook.

GRAMMAR: Negative Statements with the Verb Be

1

Short form: She's not here.

Long form: She is not here.

She's not here.

2. To make a negative statement with the verb **be**, add **not** after the verb.

3. Here are more examples:

a. My friends are not painters.
b. Ana's not from China.
c. They're not doctors.

d. He's not sick.
e. I'm not nervous.

4. Make negative sentences with the verb **be**.

a.

He's not tired.

b.

c.

d.

e.

f.

g.

h.

The answers are on page 271.

5. Negative sentences with the verb **be** have two possible short forms, except when the pronoun is **I**.
It's not necessary for you to be able to use both forms, but you should be able to recognize them when you hear them.

a. You're not tired.	or	You aren't tired.
b. He's not tired.		He isn't tired.
c. She's not tired.		She isn't tired.
d. Ana's not tired.		Ana isn't tired.
e. We're not tired.		We aren't tired.
f. They're not tired.		They aren't tired.

PRONUNCIATION: Affirmative vs. Negative

Negative sentences like 1b and 2b might be confused with affirmative sentences like 1a and 2a.

She's tired.

She isn't tired.

He's worried.

He isn't worried.

Listen to each sentence that the teacher says.
What do you hear, a or b?
Write a or b.

3.____4.____5.____6.____7.____8.____9.____10.____11.____

CONVERSATION: Getting a Prescription Filled

Su Ping Wong,
pharmacist

Mrs. Brown,
customer

First, look at ALL the pictures.
Then look at EACH picture.
WHAT IS THE PERSON SAYING? TRY TO GUESS.

Words for the Conversation on page 175.

USEFUL INFORMATION: Prescription Drugs

1. Certain drugs are called prescription drugs.
According to the law,

2. the pharmacist can't sell these without a prescription from a doctor.

3. The doctor writes a prescription and you take it to the pharmacy.

4. The prescription tells when you should take the drug and how much to take.

5. The pharmacist types this on a label and puts the label on the drug container.

6. Prescription drugs are only for the person whose name is on the label.

7. It is dangerous for another person to take a drug prescribed for you.

8. Keep your drugs out of reach of children.

9. Don't use drugs that have been in your house for a long time.

10. Some prescriptions can be renewed. Ask your pharmacist to call your doctor.

11. When you pay for your drugs, keep the receipt.

12. When you pay income tax, you may be able to claim the cost of drugs.

For sources of more information about life in Ontario, see page 269.

173

READING: Instruction Labels for Drugs

Here are some examples of doctors' instructions for taking drugs.

1-2 tablets every 4 hours.

Take 1 tablet each morning.

Sometimes the pharmacist puts another label on the drug container with more instructions. This label is usually coloured.

KEEP OUT OF REACH OF CHILDREN

Read each label below. Put an X beside every sentence under the label that is not true or not right. Put a check ✓ beside every sentence that is true or right.

1. **KEEP OUT OF REACH OF CHILDREN**

a. Your child can drink this. **X**
b. Put this where your child can't touch it. **✓**

2.  **FOR EXTERNAL USE ONLY**

a. You can drink this. ___
b. You can use this in your eyes. ___

3.  **POISON**

a. Keep this out of reach of children. ___
b. You can drink this. ___

4. **IMPORTANT** FINISH **ALL THIS MEDICATION** UNLESS OTHERWISE DIRECTED BY PRESCRIBER

a. Stop taking this drug when you feel good. ___

5.  MEDICATION SHOULD BE TAKEN WITH PLENTY OF **WATER**

a. Drink a lot of water when you take this. ___

6.  **TAKE WITH FOOD OR MILK**

a. Take this with water. ___
b. You can take this with a banana. ___

7.  **SHAKE WELL** BEFORE USING

a. One shake is enough to mix this drug. ___

8. REFRIGERATE-SHAKE WELL Discard after _Oct. 85_

a. Keep this cold. ___
b. You can take this in November /85. ___

9.  Take Medication On An EMPTY STOMACH 1 Hour Before or 2 to 3 Hours After a Meal Unless Otherwise Directed By Your Doctor.

a. Take this with food. ___
b. You ate lunch at 12:00 o'clock. It's 1:30 now. You can take this drug. ___

All the sentences in numbers 10 to 15 refer to the whole period of time that you are taking the drug.

10. **DO NOT DRINK** ALCOHOLIC BEVERAGES when taking this medication

a. You can drink wine. __
b. You can drink milk. __

11. **DO NOT** DRINK MILK OR EAT DAIRY PRODUCTS WHILE TAKING THIS MEDICATION

a. You can eat cheese. __
b. You can eat fruit. __

12. AVOID PROLONGED EXPOSURE TO SUNLIGHT While taking this medication

a. You can stay in the sun for a long time. __

13. May Cause DROWSINESS ALCOHOL may INTENSIFY this effect. USE CARE when operating a car or dangerous machinery.

a. This drug can make you sleepy. __
b. You can drink wine and then drive a car. __
c. You can drink liquor and then work on a machine. __

14. IT MAY BE ADVISABLE TO DRINK A FULL GLASS OF ORANGE JUICE OR EAT A BANANA DAILY WHILE TAKING THIS MEDICATION.

a. Eat a banana or drink a full glass of orange juice every day. __

15. OBTAIN MEDICAL ADVICE before taking non-prescription drugs as some may affect the action of this medication.

a. You can take aspirin if you like. __
b. Ask your doctor before you take any non-prescription drugs. __

The answers are on page 271.

WORDS FOR THE CONVERSATION

1. Can I help you?
2. Yes. I'd like this prescription filled.
3. Can I wait for it?
4. Yes. It'll be ready in about five minutes.
5. How much will it cost?
6. Five ninety-five.
7. Your prescription is ready.
8. How do I take it?
9. One tablet three times daily.

Other Sentences You May Hear

Picture 2: I'd like to have this prescription filled.
Picture 3: Will it take long?
Picture 5: How much will it be?

GRAMMAR: Questions with   Will

1. In sentence a, we use **will** to ask a question about the future.
   In sentences b and c, we use **will** or **'ll** to show certainty.

a

How much will my prescription cost?

b

It'll cost $5.95.

c

It'll be ready in about five minutes.

2. In a question, **will** comes before the subject. The verb, that is the base form, comes after the subject.

		SUBJECT	VERB	
How much	will	my prescription	cost?	
	Will	it	take	long?
When	will	it	be	ready?

3. Make questions with **will**.

a.

<u>When will my bicycle be ready?</u>
<u>How much will it cost?</u>

b.

<u>When will my shoes be ready?</u>
<u>How much will they cost?</u>

c.

___ ___ ___ ___ ___

___ ___ ___

d.

___ ___ ___ ___ ___

___ ___ ___

e.

___ ___ ___ ___ ___

___ ___ ___

f.

___ ___ ___ ___ ___

___ ___ ___ ___

The answers are on page 271.

UNIT 22: SUBJECTS AT SCHOOL

BEFORE THE CONVERSATION: David's Progress Report

VOCABULARY: For the Conversation

Mr. Wong

Mrs. Wong

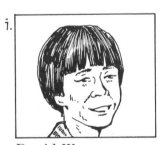

David Wong

marks

parent-teacher interview

CONVERSATION: A Parent-Teacher Interview

First, look at ALL the pictures. Then look at EACH picture.
WHAT IS THE PERSON SAYING? TRY TO GUESS.

Words for the Conversation on page 181.

USEFUL INFORMATION: Education in Ontario

1. Children between the ages of six and sixteen

2. must go to school, under Ontario law.

3. Elementary school includes kindergarten and grades 1 to 8.

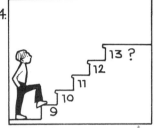

4. Secondary school includes grades 9 to 12 and possibly a fifth year.

5. A student can complete secondary school in 4, 4½ or 5 years.*

6. A subject can be at different levels of difficulty.

7. For example, English can be basic, general or advanced.

8. The student should choose subjects and levels

9. that he or she will need for employment or further education.

10. The parent and the teacher, principal or guidance counsellor

11. can help guide the student in choosing subjects and levels.

12. Universities provide post-secondary education. They charge fees.

*For more information, contact your local school board.

13.

If you need help to pay the fees, you can ask for a grant or loan at the university.

14.

Colleges of applied arts and technology also provide post-secondary education. Their fees are lower.

15.

Adults can study secondary school subjects part-time or

16.

at home through correspondence courses.*

SPEAKING ACTIVITY

Take a partner. Ask your partner about education in his or her country. Below are some questions you can ask. Write your partner's answers.

1. At what age does a child begin school? _____

2. At what age does a student usually leave school? _____

3. Is education free? _____

4. How many students are there usually in a class? _____

5. Do children have homework in elementary schools? _____

6. Do parents go to the school to talk to the teachers? _____

7. Do many people finish secondary school? _____

8. Is it easy or difficult to go to university? _____

*For more information, see page 208.

READING AND WRITING: Notes From Home

Here are some notes that parents might send to the teacher at school.

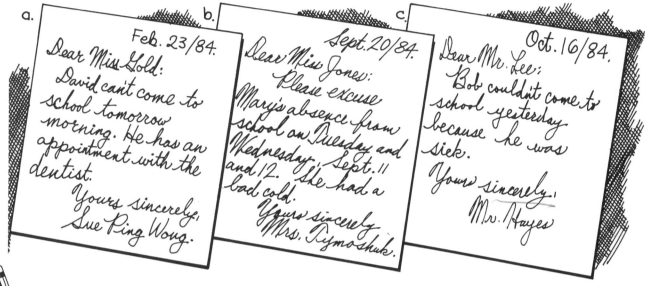

a.
Feb. 23/84.
Dear Miss Gold:
David can't come to school tomorrow morning. He has an appointment with the dentist.
Yours sincerely,
Sue Ping Wong.

b.
Sept. 20/84.
Dear Miss Jones:
Please excuse Mary's absence from school on Tuesday and Wednesday, Sept. 11 and 12. She had a bad cold.
Yours sincerely
Mrs. Tymoshuk.

c.
Oct. 16/84.
Dear Mr. Lee:
Bob couldn't come to school yesterday because he was sick.
Yours sincerely,
Mr. Hayes

In your notebook, write a note that a parent might send to a teacher.

WORDS FOR THE CONVERSATION

1. Mr. and Mrs. Wong? Come in please.
2. How is David getting on in school?
3. Fine.
4. He has eighties and nineties. Those are good marks.
5. His mark in math isn't good. He got fifty-four.
6. Don't worry.
7. He's improving.
8. How can we help?
9. See that he does his homework.
10. Bye. Thank you very much.

Other Sentences You May Hear

Picture 2: How is David doing?
Picture 3: Very well.
Picture 7: He's getting better.
Picture 8: What can we do to help?
Picture 9: Make sure that he does his homework.

VOCABULARY: For the Reading

Part I: Some School Subjects

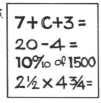

1. English
2. French
3. Mathematics
4. History
5. Geography
6. Science
7. Family Studies
8. Art
9. Industrial Arts
10. Music
11. Physical Education

Part II: Other Words and Symbols Used on a Progress Report

ACHIEVEMENT

Achievement is sometimes shown in elementary school by letters: A, B, C, D or E. A is the highest.

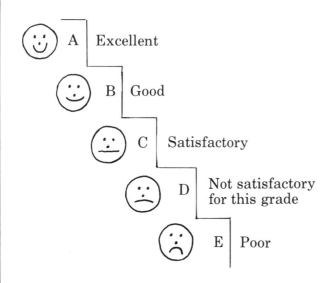

A — Excellent

B — Good

C — Satisfactory

D — Not satisfactory for this grade

E — Poor

EFFORT

Your child's effort is shown by the teacher's comments and sometimes by letters. Here is what the letters mean.

O = Outstanding

S = Satisfactory

U = Unsatisfactory

182

READING: An Achievement or Progress Report

SURNAME Wong	GIVEN NAMES David		CLASS 9 B	DATE Mar. 8/84
SUBJECT	ACHIEVEMENT	EFFORT	COMMENTS	
1. English	82	S		
2. French	87	O	David really enjoys French *J.P.*	
3. Math	54	U	Needs to do more Homework. *TR*	
4. History	91	O	David seems to read a lot about history *TR*	
5. Geography	72	S		
6. Science	86	S		
7. Family Studies	80	S		
8. Art	90	O	David excels in art. He has a lot of talent. *TR*	
9. Industrial Art	73	S		
10. Music	70	S	David could listen more carefully in class. *a.L.*	
11. Physical Education	79	S		

Answer these questions in your notebook.

a. In what six subjects did David get eighties and nineties?
b. In what subject did David get fifty-four?
c. Which two subjects does David seem to like very much?
d. In which subject does David have a lot of talent?
e. In which subject does David need to listen more carefully in class?
f. In which subject does David need to put more effort and work harder at home?

The answers are on page 271.

GRAMMAR: Do or Does as the Main Verb

A

In this sentence **does** is a helping verb or auxiliary. **Live** is the main verb.

He doesn't live on Queen Street.

B

In this sentence the main verb is **does**.

See that he does his homework.

Here are more examples of **does** or **do** as an auxiliary verb.
What is the main verb in each case?

1. I don't **know** the time.
2. Do you **have** a pencil?
3. Does this bus **go** to Queen St.
4. What time does the store **open** on Monday?
5. They don't **like** spaghetti.

Here are more examples of **does** or **do** as a main verb.

6. What kind of work do you **do**?
7. I **do** many different things.
8. What kind of work did you **do** in Portugal?
9. I **do** the laundry on Tuesdays.
10. He **does** the shopping on Saturdays.
11. She **does** the laundry on Mondays.

Make sentences. Use **do** or **does** as the main verb.

a.

We do the dishes at 7 o'clock.

b.

I do my hair on Fridays.

c.

——— ——— ———

d.

——— ——— ———

e.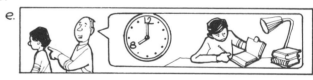

——— ——— ———

f.

——— ——— ———

g.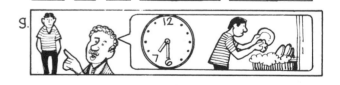

——— ——— ———

h.

——— ——— ———

The answers are on page 271.

UNIT 23: INVITATION

PHOTO STORY: A Neighbour Invites Ana in for Coffee

6

7

8

9

186

DIALOGUES WITH CHOICES

Take a partner. One of you is A; the other one is B. Person A says one sentence, for example, number 1. Person B responds with one sentence, for example, number 3.

You can make a new dialogue by choosing different sentences, for example, numbers 2 and 4. You can also make a new dialogue by changing the word(s) in the brackets. Just below the pictures are words that you can put into the brackets. For example, you can say: "It's a beautiful (morning), isn't it?"

Make as many dialogues as you can. Then switch with your partner.

I. Talking about the Good Weather

A   1. It's a beautiful (day), isn't it?
2. Isn't it a beautiful (day)?

B   3. Yes. I hope it's like this on the weekend.
4. Yes. I hope it stays like this on the weekend.

a 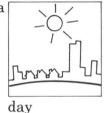 b 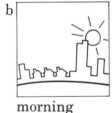 c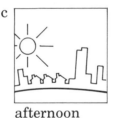

day   morning   afternoon

II. Compliments

A 5. Your (garden) looks beautiful.
6. Your (garden) looks great. INFORMAL

B 7. Thank you. FORMAL
8. Thanks. INFORMAL

d  e  f

garden   hair   cake

III. Invitations

A 9. Do you have time for coffee? I'm having some. INFORMAL
10. Would like to come in for coffee? FORMAL

B 11. Sure. That would be nice.
12. Yes. That sounds nice.

IV. Suggestions

A 13. Let's sit in (the kitchen). It's cool in there.
14. Why don't we sit in (the kitchen)?

B 15. Okay. Good idea. INFORMAL
16. That's a good idea.

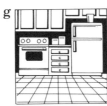  

g the kitchen h the living room i the dining room

V. Offers

A 17. Would you like some (cake)? FORMAL
18. Do you want some (cake)? INFORMAL

B 19. Yes, please.

j cake k coffee l tea m ice-cream

VI. Compliments

A 20. This (cake) is very good.
21. I like this (cake).
22. I really like this (cake).

B 23. Thank you.
24. I'm glad you like it.
25. Thanks. Would you like some more?

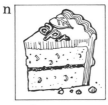   

n cake o coffee p tea q ice-cream

PHOTOS WITHOUT WORDS

Here are the photographs from the photo story. Can you remember what the people are saying?

SPEAKING ACTIVITY WITH CHOICES

Take a partner. One of you is A. The other one is B. Follow each set of instructions below and make as many conversations as you can. Then switch with your partner.

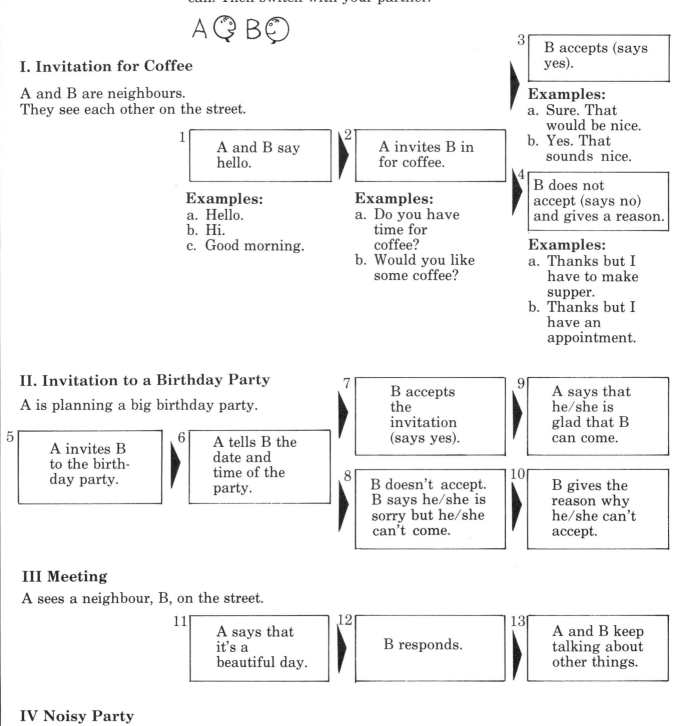

I. Invitation for Coffee

A and B are neighbours.
They see each other on the street.

1 A and B say hello.

Examples:
a. Hello.
b. Hi.
c. Good morning.

2 A invites B in for coffee.

Examples:
a. Do you have time for coffee?
b. Would you like some coffee?

3 B accepts (says yes).

Examples:
a. Sure. That would be nice.
b. Yes. That sounds nice.

4 B does not accept (says no) and gives a reason.

Examples:
a. Thanks but I have to make supper.
b. Thanks but I have an appointment.

II. Invitation to a Birthday Party

A is planning a big birthday party.

5 A invites B to the birthday party.

6 A tells B the date and time of the party.

7 B accepts the invitation (says yes).

8 B doesn't accept. B says he/she is sorry but he/she can't come.

9 A says that he/she is glad that B can come.

10 B gives the reason why he/she can't accept.

III Meeting

A sees a neighbour, B, on the street.

11 A says that it's a beautiful day.

12 B responds.

13 A and B keep talking about other things.

IV Noisy Party

A and B are neighbours. A is having a party and the music is turned up very high. B can't sleep because of the loud music. B gets out of bed and knocks on A's door.

READING: The Weather and Temperature

Look at these words and pictures.

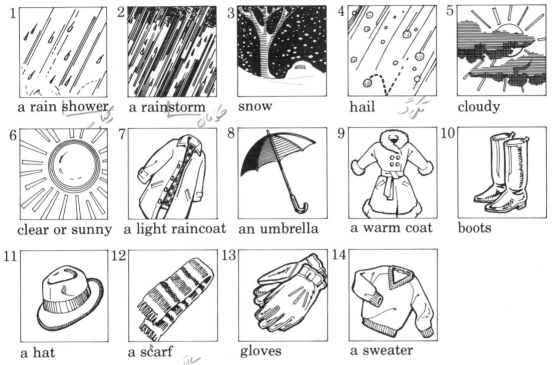

1   a rain shower   2   a rainstorm   3   snow   4   hail   5   cloudy

6   clear or sunny   7   a light raincoat   8   an umbrella   9   a warm coat   10   boots

11   a hat   12   a scarf   13   gloves   14   a sweater

Now read each weather forecast and circle the items you will take
when you go outside.

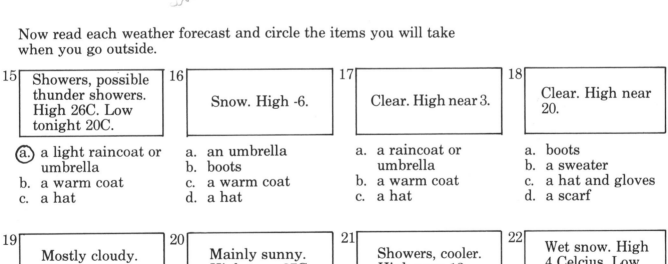

15 Showers, possible thunder showers. High 26C. Low tonight 20C.

   (a.) a light raincoat or umbrella
   b. a warm coat
   c. a hat

16 Snow. High -6.

   a. an umbrella
   b. boots
   c. a warm coat
   d. a hat

17 Clear. High near 3.

   a. a raincoat or umbrella
   b. a warm coat
   c. a hat

18 Clear. High near 20.

   a. boots
   b. a sweater
   c. a hat and gloves
   d. a scarf

19 Mostly cloudy. High near -1.

   a. a warm coat
   b. a sweater
   c. a hat and scarf
   d. gloves

20 Mainly sunny. High near 27C.

   a. a warm coat
   b. gloves
   c. a hat
   d. a scarf

21 Showers, cooler. High near 13.

   a. a raincoat
   b. an umbrella
   c. a sweater
   d. a scarf

22 Wet snow. High 4 Celcius. Low tonight -4C.

   a. boots
   b. a sweater
   c. a warm coat
   d. a scarf

USEFUL INFORMATION: Daylight Saving Time

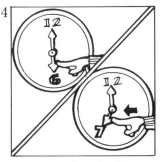

Spring begins towards the end of March.

In spring, the days are longer. There are more hours of daylight.

On the last Sunday in April

we turn the clock ahead one hour.

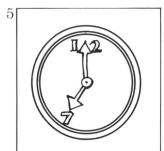

This new time is called daylight saving time.

We wake up earlier and get one extra hour of daylight.

Fall begins towards the end of September.

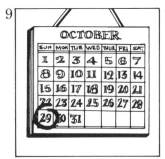

In the fall the nights are longer.

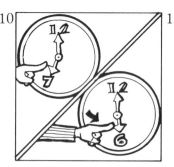

On the last Sunday in October

we turn the clock back one hour.

Daylight saving time is over. We are back to standard time.

GRAMMAR AND PRONUNCIATION: The Possessive

1

In this sentence,
your
is a possessive adjective.

Your garden looks
beautiful.

2. Here are the possessive adjectives.

a. **my**   b. **your**   c. **his**   d. **her**   e. **our**   f. **their**

3. Make sentences. Begin each sentence with **This is**.

a. **This is his first job.**

b. **This is their car.**

c.   f.   i.

The answers are on page 271.

4. **Her** and **your** can sound almost the same.
Listen to each sentence that the teacher says.
Which possessive adjective do you hear, a or b?

a **her**   b **your**

1 _____ 2 _____ 3 _____ 4 _____ 5 _____ 6 _____ 7 _____ 8 _____ 9 _____

5. If we have a noun, we add **'s** to show possession.
This is Ana's first job.   Ana likes Jean's garden.

CULTURAL DISCUSSION: Neighbours

Read this passage.

> Ana's neighbour Jean is very friendly. She invited Ana in for coffee.
>
> Not all neighbours are so friendly. Some neighbours will not talk to you at all.
>
> Sometimes neighbours will talk to you on the street but not invite you to their homes. But people with children often get to know other people on the street who have children.
>
> In apartment buildings you may not even see your neighbours for weeks.
>
> People in a small town are usually more friendly than people in a big city.

Are the statements below true or false? Circle a. or b.

1 All neighbours talk to you. a. true b. false

2 Usually neighbours who talk to you on the street will invite you to their homes. a. true b. false

3 People with children are often friendly towards other people with children. a. true b. false

The answers are on page 271.

Talk about your neighbours in your native country. The questions below will help you. Here are some verbs in the past tense that you might need.

1 invited	7 didn't invite
2 talked	8 didn't talk
3 spoke	9 didn't speak
4 saw	10 didn't see
5 liked	11 didn't like
6 got to know	12 didn't get to know

Where did you live (in a house, a room, or an apartment)?
Were your neighbours friendly?
Which ones were friendly?
How often did you see them?
Did you talk to your neighbours?
If not, why not?
What did you talk about?
Did you visit in one another's homes?

  Talk about your neighbours in Canada.

UNIT 24: SOCIAL VISIT

PHOTO STORY: Ana and Her Neighbours

1

2

3

4

5

6 I'm thinking of taking a course at night school.

7 What kind of course?

I'm not sure yet.

8 How about another piece of cake?

No thanks. It's delicious but I'm having supper soon.

9 Oh. Look at the time. I have to go now. I'm expecting some friends.

10 Thanks for the cake and coffee.

You're welcome. I'm glad you could drop in.

DIALOGUES WITH CHOICES

See instructions on page 187.

I. Asking About People

A 1. How are your (children)?

B 2. They're fine. They're both at day camp this summer.

children   sisters   brothers

II. Offers

A 3. How about (another piece of cake)? INFORMAL
4. Would you like (another piece of cake)? FORMAL

B 5. No thanks. It's delicious but I'm having supper soon.
6. No thanks. It's good but I've had enough.
7. Yes, please.

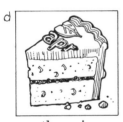   

another piece   another cup   another cup   more ice-cream
of cake   of coffee   of tea

III. Expressing Thanks

A 8. Thanks for the cake and coffee.
9. Thanks. I enjoyed that.
10. That was a nice visit.

B 11. You're welcome. I'm glad you could drop in. FORMAL
12. Bye. Drop in again. INFORMAL
13. Bye. See you soon. INFORMAL

PHOTOS WITHOUT WORDS

Here are the photographs from the photo story. Can you remember what the people are saying?

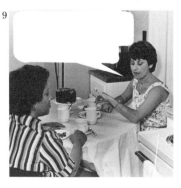

SPEAKING ACTIVITY WITH CHOICES

Take a partner. One of you is A. The other one is B. Follow each set of instructions below and make as many conversations as you can. Then switch with your partner.

A 😮   B 😮

I. Telephone Call

B is calling A on the telephone.
A's telephone is ringing.

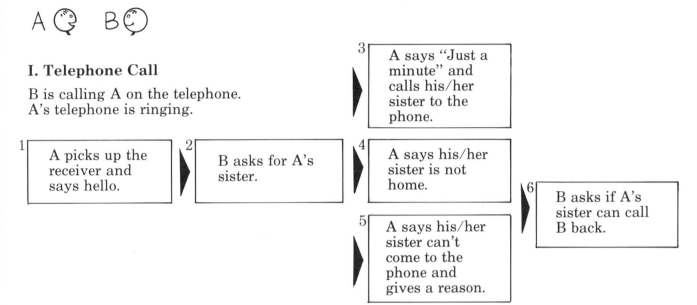

1 | A picks up the receiver and says hello.

2 | B asks for A's sister.

3 | A says "Just a minute" and calls his/her sister to the phone.

4 | A says his/her sister is not home.

5 | A says his/her sister can't come to the phone and gives a reason.

6 | B asks if A's sister can call B back.

II. Friendly Enquiry

A meets a friend, B, on the street. A hasn't seen B for a long time.

7 | A and B say hello.

8 | A asks what B is doing these days.

9 | B answers.

10 | A and B keep the conversation going.

III. Compliments

A is eating at the house of a friend, B.

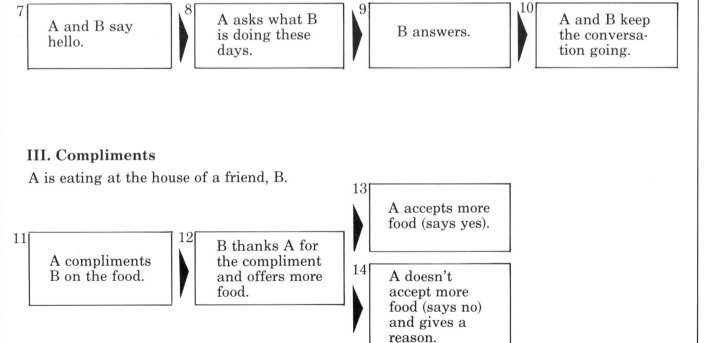

11 | A compliments B on the food.

12 | B thanks A for the compliment and offers more food.

13 | A accepts more food (says yes).

14 | A doesn't accept more food (says no) and gives a reason.

199

GRAMMAR: The Present Continuous Tense

1. In this sentence from photo number 3 the verb **take** is in the present continuous or present progressive tense. The action of the verb is in the present.

Short form: He's taking a shower.
Long form: He is taking a shower.

2. To write the present continuous tense, take the base form of the verb, remove **e**, add **ing** and use the verb **be** as an auxiliary.

3. Here are more examples.

Ana's thinking of taking a course.   She's expecting some friends.
We're watching television.   They're reading.

4. Make sentences. Use the present continuous tense.

He's taking a shower.

5. With some verbs, we can use the present continuous for a future action which we anticipate in the present.

I'm having supper soon.

6. Make sentences about the future. Use the present continuous tense.

They're having supper at six o'clock.

The answers are on page 271.

CULTURAL DISCUSSION: Summer Holidays

Read this passage.

> In the summer holidays, when school is closed, children do different things.
>
> Some children go to summer camp. This is out of town, in the country. Children leave home for one or two weeks or more and stay at the camp. They go swimming, boating, hiking, etc.
>
> Not everyone has enough money to send their children to summer camp. Sometimes a newspaper or a community organization will collect money to pay for children who want to go to camp but who don't have enough money.
>
> Day camp is different. When children go to day camp they come back home each day. Sometimes community centres or churches have day camps. The children do many things, for example: visit the museum or art gallery, go swimming, make pictures or crafts, play in the park. Day camp costs money too, but it's not usually expensive.

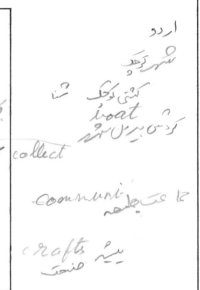

Listen to some statements. For each one, write **true** or **false** in your notebook.

Talk about children in your native country. What do they do when they don't go to school?

PRONUNCIATION: Markings on Stressed Syllables

In some dictionaries, this mark ' comes before the syllable that has the strongest stress.

children   'child ren

Listen to each word below. Mark the syllable with the strongest stress.

1. summer   'sum mer   5. something   some thing
2. another   an oth er   6. better   bet ter
3. shower   show er   7. delicious   de li cious
4. expecting   ex pect ing   8. welcome   wel come
                                              9. supper   sup per

The answers are on page 271.

PHOTO STORY: Ana Talks to Her Employer

5

6

7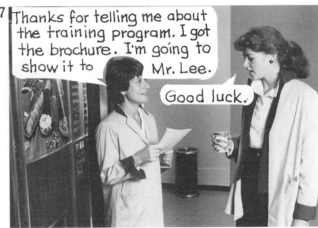

8

DIALOGUES WITH CHOICES

Take a partner. One of you is A; the other one is B. Person A says one sentence, for example, number 1. Person B responds with one sentence, for example, number 3.
You can make a new dialogue by choosing different sentences, for example, numbers 2 and 4. You can also make a new dialogue by changing the word(s) in the brackets. You can choose from the words in capital letters. For example, you can say: "How can I find out about (evening courses)?"
Make as many dialogues as you can. Then switch with your partner.

I. Asking for Information

A 1. How can I find out about (special training for women)?
2. Where can I get information about (special training for women)?

B 3. Go to a Canada Employment Centre.
4. Ask at a Community Information Centre.*

| SPECIAL TRAINING FOR WOMEN | EVENING COURSES | CORRESPONDENCE COURSES | COURSES FOR UNEMPLOYED PEOPLE |

II. Asking to Talk to Someone

A 5. Can I talk to you for a few minutes? It's about (the job ad).
6. Can I see you for a few minutes? It's about (the job ad).

B 7. Sure. Come in and sit down.
8. Can you come back later?
9. I'm busy today. Can you see me tomorrow?

THE JOB AD   MY PAY CHEQUE   MY VACATION

III. Telling How Long You've Been Here

A 10. I've been here (for three months).

B 11. Well. Don't give up. There'll be other jobs.
12. Well. Keep trying. There'll be other jobs.

| FOR THREE MONTHS | FOR SIX MONTHS | FOR A YEAR | FOR TWO YEARS |

*Some centres are listed in the Appendix of the "Newcomers Guide to Services in Ontario" published by the Ontario Ministry of Citizenship and Culture.

PHOTOS WITHOUT WORDS

Here are some photographs from the photo story. Can you remember what the people are saying?

SPEAKING ACTIVITY WITH CHOICES

Take a partner. One of you is A. The other one is B. Follow each set of instructions below and make as many conversations as you can. Then switch with your partner.

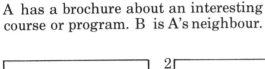

I. Asking for Help

A has a brochure about an interesting course or program. B is A's neighbour.

1 | A tells B that he/she got a brochure and what it is about.

2 | A tells B that it's difficult to understand and A asks if B can help him/her.

3 | B says yes and invites A into his/her house.

4 | B says that he/she can't help now and gives the reason.

5 | B asks if A can come back later and suggests another time.

II. Asking to Speak to Someone

A has a job. B is A's employer.

6 | A asks to talk to B.

7 | A tells B what it's about.

8 | B says yes and invites A in to sit down.

9 | B says that he/she can't talk now.

10 | A says that it's very important and it will only take a few minutes.

11 | B asks if A can come back later; B suggests another time.

III. Asking For a Job Training Course

Do this section later after you have completed the whole unit.
A is at a Canada Employment Centre. B is the counsellor.

12 | A says that he/she would like to apply for a job training course.

13 | A says that he/she tried and tried but can't find a job.

14 | A says that he/she has a job, but would like to train for a better job.

15 | B asks what kind of job A would like.

16 | A is not sure, and would like to see a list of courses.

17 | A tells B exactly what kind of job he/she would like.

207

READING: Courses for Job Upgrading

Let's say that you want to get a job, or a better job, like Ana. You need better job skills; you need to take a course. The government gives many courses that are free or not too expensive.

NAME OF PROGRAM	KIND OF TRAINING	FINANCES	WHERE TO ENQUIRE
1. Manpower courses (National Institutional Training)	classroom courses for: waitress, bartender, furniture upholsterer, etc. etc. English, etc. etc.	free courses You get money to live on while you study.	a Canada Employment Centre
2. Post-secondary courses	daytime or evening classroom courses for: nurse, machinist, secretary, the theatre, etc. etc.	fees not expensive	a community college (a College of Applied Arts and Technology) or your local school board
3. General Industrial Training	on the job courses for: dressmaker, jeweller, welder, electrical repairing, etc. etc.	Canada Employment pays the employer part of your salary while you work and learn	Go to a Canada Employment Centre for a list of courses. Ask an employer if he/she can train you.
4. Apprenticeship Programs	for a licence in a highly skilled job: mechanic, electrician, plumber, etc. etc.	You get a salary while you work and learn.	Apprenticeship Branch of the Ministry of Colleges and Universities
5. Adult education courses	daytime or evening, secondary school grades 9-13	free or inexpensive	your local school board
6. Ontario Ministry of Education correspondence courses	at home, secondary school grades 9-13	free	The Ontario Ministry of Education

Some of this information came from the book, "Making Changes: Employment Orientation for Immigrant Women" published by the Cross Cultural Communication Centre in Toronto.

Answer these questions:

1. You are unemployed and you would like to become a bartender. Where do you go to ask about courses?
2. You would like to get an electrician's licence and earn a salary while you learn. Where do you go to ask about this?
3. You have been working on an assembly board in the same electronics factory for 1½ years.
   a. You would like to do something more interesting, but you don't know what courses are possible for you. Where do you go to find out?
   b. You would like to learn electrical repairing. Who can you speak to about training on the job?
4. You didn't complete secondary school in your country and you would like to study at home on Saturday and Sunday to get your secondary school grades. What program are you looking for?

The answers are on page 272.

GRAMMAR: Object Forms of Pronouns

1. In this sentence, the pronoun **I** is subject of the verb **ask**. The pronoun **me** refers to the same person as **I**, but is the object form. It is object of the verb **help**.

   SUBJECT   VERB OBJECT VERB OBJECT

I'll have to ask Jean to help me.

2. Here are the object forms of the pronouns. The subject forms are in brackets.

me (I)	you (you)	him (he)	her (she)	us (we)	them (they)	it (it)	them (they)

3. Write the object form of each missing person.

 a. I'm glad you like _it_

 c. Can you tell _me_ the time?

 e. We'll give _them_ the information.

 b. Please give _her_ this message.

 d. I'll ask _him_ to help me.

 f. I'll buy _them_

209

GRAMMAR: Going to   with a Verb

1. In this sentence, Ana is talking about a future action. She is expressing her intention.

Short form: I'm going to show it to Mr. Lee.

Long form: I am going to show it to Mr. Lee.

2. For intentions we can use **going to** with the base form of the verb and the verb be as the auxiliary.

I'm You're He/She's Ana's We're They're	going to	show it to Mr. Lee. apply for that job. have some coffee. watch television tonight. take a course in September. eat supper at 7 o'clock.

3. Make a sentence with each verb below. Using **going to**.

BUY   EAT   VISIT   READ   WATCH TELEVISION

CULTURAL DISCUSSION: Women Working

Read this passage.

> There are special government programs to help women advance in their work. For example, in the General Industrial Training program, the government sometimes gives the employer money specifically for the training of women.
>
> Some community centres offer special courses for women who want to improve their job skills. These courses might be at the Y.W.C.A., at a library, at a multicultural or cross cultural centre, or at a community college.
>
> Working women are also protected by the law.* When a woman applies for a job, the employer must give her the same chance that a man would get, except in special cases.
>
> People who are working might need to put their young children in daycare. This costs money. The government allows tax deductions for daycare costs, when there is no parent at home to be with the children.

 Listen to some statements. For each one, write **true** or **false** in your notebook.

 Talk about working women in your native country.

*You can read about the Ontario Human Rights Code on page 258 and about the Employment Standards Act on page 250.

UNIT 26: UNEMPLOYMENT INSURANCE

PHOTO STORY: Tony is Out of Work

1 I'm sorry, Tony. When this job is finished, I won't have any more work for you.

I understand. I'm pretty sure I'll find another job.

2 Well, that's it. By the way, have you found another job?

No. Not yet. I'm going to the Canada Employment Centre tomorrow.

3 Here's your Record of Employment. You'll need it for unemployment insurance benefits.

Thanks. Let's keep in touch.

4 May I help you?

Yes. I've been laid off. I'd like to apply for unemployment insurance benefits.

15 Well, not right now. There are no painting jobs either. If anything comes in we'll call you.

I'd appreciate that.

16 Well, you have worked enough weeks to qualify for benefits. You know, of course, that it's up to you to keep looking for work.

Yes, I understand that.

17 Keep a record of where you look for work. Don't forget to come in and check the Job Boards.

Okay.

18 You'll receive a card like this every two weeks. Fill it out and mail it back right away.

19 You can call this number if you have any problems.

Thank you.

DIALOGUES WITH CHOICES

See instructions on page 205.

I. Asking Someone If They've Had Any Luck

A 1. Have you found (another job)?
  2. Have you had any luck finding (another job)?

  B 3. No. Not yet. I'm going to the Canada Employment Centre tomorrow.
    4. Yes. As a matter of fact, I have.

ANOTHER   A JOB AS A   A TEACHING
JOB   MUSICIAN   JOB

II. Applying for Something

A 5. May I help you? VERY FORMAL
  6. Can I help you? FORMAL

  B 7. Yes. I'd like to apply for (unemployment insurance benefits).

UNEMPLOYMENT   A JOB   A TRAINING
INSURANCE   COURSE
BENEFITS

III. Suggestions

A 8. You can take a look (at the Job Boards).
  9. Why don't you take a look (at the Job Boards)?

  B 10. Thank you. I will. FORMAL
    11. Thanks. I will. INFORMAL

AT THE JOB   IN THE   AT THE
BOARDS   NEWSPAPER   BULLETIN
                                     BOARD

PHOTOS WITHOUT WORDS

Here are some photographs from the photo story.
Can you remember what the people are saying?

216

SPEAKING ACTIVITY WITH CHOICES

Take a partner. One of you is A. The other one is B. Follow each set of instructions below and make as many conversations as you can. Then switch with your partner.

 A  B

I. Saying Goodbye

A has been working or studying with B and now the job or course is finished.

| 1. A suggests to B that they keep in touch. | 2. A gives his/her phone number to B and asks B to call him/her some time. | 3. B thanks A. | 4. B gives A his/her phone number. |

II. Getting in Touch

A and B are the same people as above. A little time has passed and A is calling B on the telephone.

| 5. B says hello. | 6. A says his/her name. "This is ___." | 7. A and B ask each other how they are. | 8. A invites B for something. |

9. B accepts and would be glad to come.

10. B can't come and gives a reason why.

11. B can't come and suggests another time for meeting.

III. Directions

A is on his/her way to a Canada Employment Centre. A has just gotten off the bus and can't find the street. A sees B, a friendly-looking person.

| 12. A stops B. "Excuse me." | 13. A asks where ___ Street is. | 14. B says he/she doesn't know. | 15. B asks what A is looking for. | 16. A answers. | 17. B knows where it is and gives directions. |

Make a new conversation by changing the place you are looking for.
Ask for a place in your own area, instead of the Canada Employment Centre.

READING AND WRITING: Application for U.I. Benefits

Here are some questions from the form that Tony filled out at the Canada Employment Centre.

D WORK DESIRED						
24 Are you ready and willing	☐ *No* ☑ Yes	If no, explain and give date you will be available		D	M	Y
If yes, (a) are there any days you can't work?	☑ No ☐ Yes	If yes, specify				
(b) Are there any hours each day you can't work?	☑ No ☐ Yes	If yes, specify				

25. INDICATE THE TYPE OF WORK YOU ARE SEEKING	Years of experience	Salary desired
Type		
piano or clarinet : teaching or playing	one	$16.00 an hr.
house painting, furniture moving	three months	$7.00 an hr.

26 In what geographical areas, municipality, town or province are you personally seeking work?

close to Toronto

Answer these questions in your notebook.

1. Does Tony want to start work now?
2. On which days can Tony work?
3. During which hours can Tony work?
4. What kind of music work does Tony want?
5. What other kind of work is he willing to do?
6. In music, how much money does Tony want to earn?
7. Where does Tony want to work?

The answers are on page 272.

Now answer these questions for yourself.

D WORK DESIRED						
24 Are you ready and willing	☐ *No* ☐ Yes	If no, explain and give date you will be available		D	M	Y
If yes, (a) are there any days you can't work?	☐ No ☐ Yes	If yes, specify				
(b) Are there any hours each day you can't work?	☐ No ☐ Yes	If yes, specify				

25. INDICATE THE TYPE OF WORK YOU ARE SEEKING	Years of experience	Salary desired
Type		

26 In what geographical areas, municipality, town or province are you personally seeking work?

COMMUNICATION ACTIVITY: Interview

Take a partner. One of you is A. The other one is B.

A

 Imagine you are someone looking for a job.
Write this information in your notebook:

— your occupation
— the name of your last employer
— how long the job lasted (the starting and finishing dates)
— what type of job you are looking for now

B

You are a counsellor in a Canada Manpower Centre. Ask A these questions.

What was your last job?
Who was your employer?
How long did the job last?
What type of job are you looking for now?

 Write A's answers in your notebook.

Then check what you wrote with the information that is in your partner's notebook.

GRAMMAR: Won't

1. When this job is finished, I won't have any more work for you.

   In the sentence above from photo no. 1, Lou is expressing certainty about the future. He is making a negative prediction.

   Short form: I won't have any more work for you.

   Long form: I will not have any more work for you.

2. Here are some predictions in the affirmative.
   Make each prediction negative. Change **will** to **won't**.

   a. I'm pretty sure I'll find another job.

   I'm pretty sure I won't find another job.

   b. I'll find what I want on the job boards.
   c. Tony will get a good job.
   d. It will take ten minutes to fill this prescription.
   e. The bus will arrive at seven-thirty.

   The answers are on page 272.

CULTURAL DISCUSSION: Unemployment Insurance

Read this passage.

18 - 20

> If you have a job, you pay unemployment insurance premiums every month.
>
> If you lose your job, you can get unemployment insurance benefits, as long as you have worked for a certain number of weeks.
>
> After you apply for benefits, you have to wait for a certain minimum period of time before you get any money.
> If you left your job voluntarily, then this period is longer.
>
> There are special benefits if you get sick, have a baby or become 65 years old (even if you are still working).
> If you are self-employed, you are not eligible for unemployment insurance.

Listen to some statements. For each one, write **true** or **false** in your notebook.

Talk about people who can't work in your native country. How do they manage?

PRONUNCIATION: Markings on Stressed Syllables

In some dictionaries, this mark ′ comes after the syllable that has the strongest stress.

another   an oth′ er

Listen to each word below. Mark the syllable with the strongest stress.

1. employment   em ploy′ ment
2. tomorrow   to mor row
3. insurance   in sur ance
4. complete   com plete
5. painter   paint er
6. assistant   as sist ant

7. yesterday   yes ter day
8. nothing   noth ing
9. musician   mu si cian
10. interested   in ter est ed
11. certainly   cer tain ly

The answers are on page 272.

220

UNIT 27: LOOKING FOR WORK

PHOTO STORY: Tony Looks for a Job

1. How did it go today?

Not too good. I went to the employment centre but there were no jobs. I applied for __benefits__.

2. I'm going to look for work in a __music__ school. Where did you put the Yellow Pages?

Right over there.

3. Here's one in the area.

4. They're probably still open. I think I'll go now.

Good luck.

9

10

11

12

13

DIALOGUES WITH CHOICES

See instructions on page 205.

I. Asking How Things Went

A 1. How did things go (today)?

B 2. Not too good.
3. Not bad.
4. Very well.

TODAY   YESTERDAY   LAST WEEK

II. Asking for a Suggestion

A 5. Can you suggest another (music school) I could try?
INFORMAL
6. Could you suggest another (music school) I could try?
FORMAL

B 7. There's a small (music school) around the corner.
8. Here's the name of another (music school). They
might have an opening.

MUSIC SCHOOL   FACTORY   RESTAURANT   PHARMACY

III. Leaving Your Name

A 9. Can I leave (my name and phone number) with you
in case something comes up? INFORMAL
10. Could I leave (my name and phone number) with you
in case something comes up? FORMAL

B 11. Sure. You never know.
12. Why not? You can never tell.

MY NAME AND   MY NAME   MY BUSINESS CARD
PHONE NUMBER   AND ADDRESS

PHOTOS WITHOUT WORDS

Look at the Photo Story on pages 221 to 223 and cover up the words in these photos: 1, 2, 3, 4, 6, 7, 10, 11, 12, 13.
Can you remember what the people are saying?

SPEAKING ACTIVITY WITH CHOICES

Take a partner. One of you is A. The other one is B.
Follow each set of instructions below and make as many conversations as you can.

I. Asking for the Manager

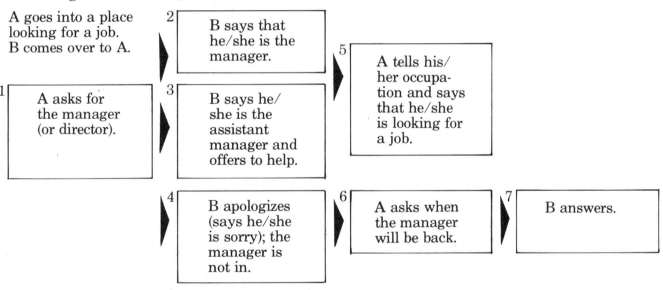

A goes into a place looking for a job. B comes over to A.

1. A asks for the manager (or director).

2. B says that he/she is the manager.

3. B says he/she is the assistant manager and offers to help.

5. A tells his/her occupation and says that he/she is looking for a job.

4. B apologizes (says he/she is sorry); the manager is not in.

6. A asks when the manager will be back.

7. B answers.

II. Asking for a Suggestion

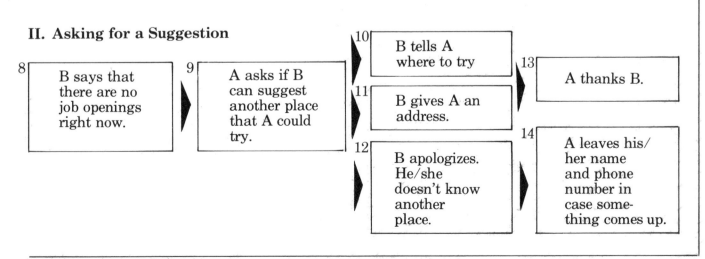

8. B says that there are no job openings right now.

9. A asks if B can suggest another place that A could try.

10. B tells A where to try

11. B gives A an address.

12. B apologizes. He/she doesn't know another place.

13. A thanks B.

14. A leaves his/her name and phone number in case something comes up.

حصہ زردرائل کا پید اکرا ں

USEFUL INFORMATION: Looking for a Job

Looking for a job can be very time-consuming. Here are some tips.

Go to a Canada Employment Centre.
Check the Job Boards, including the new listings. You can go in and do this as often as you like.
If you don't find a job on your own, ask to talk to a counsellor.

Look in the Yellow Pages.
Write down the names of several companies in your line of work. Then contact those companies and ask if there is any work for you. If not, ask them to suggest another place where you can look.

Tell your friends that you are looking for a job.
Sometimes the news of a job vacancy travels by word of mouth.

Look for advertisements.
Look in the newspaper.
You can look in the classified section under "Help Wanted".
You can also look at the "Professional" or "Careers" page.
Sometimes you can find a job ad by walking along the street. Some store owners post ads in their store windows.
Check the bulletin boards in schools, offices and community centres.
Professional or trade journals often carry ads.

Research:
1. Find a job in the newspaper or somewhere else. Cut it out or copy it. Then bring it to class and tell why you chose it. or 2. Look in the Yellow Pages and find the name of a company in your line of work. Write down the name, address and telephone number.

READING: Job Advertisements in the Newspaper

Here are some short forms that you will find in job ads. Match the long form to the short form and put the letter in the box.

1 C 1 yr.
2 D bus. exper.
3 A 60 wpm typing
4 F 20 hrs./wk
5 B salary neg.
6 G sect'y
7 E reg'd technologist
8 I lic. mechanic
9 J part-time avail.
10 H refs. required

A. 60 words per minute typing 3
B. salary negotiable قابلِ ادائیگی تنخواہ
C. one year ۱
D. business experience ۲
E. registered technologist
F. 20 hours per week ۴
G. secretary
H. references required کاغذاتِ تصدیق
I. licensed mechanic
J. part-time available

The answers are on page 272.

GRAMMAR: Two-word Verbs

1. Here is a sentence from the photo story with a two-word verb. It is underlined.

   Can I leave my name and number with you in case something <u>comes up</u>?

2. A two-word verb has a verb and a particle.

   VERB: comes

   PARTICLE: up

3. A two-word verb often has a special meaning that is not apparent when you look at the two words separately. Here is a sentence that shows the meaning of the two-word verb above.

   Can I leave my name and phone number with you in case <u>there is a job opening</u>?

4. On the left are some sentences with two-word verbs. On the right are sentences that show their meaning. The sentences on the right are more formal.

   a. Please <u>fill out</u> this application form.

   a. Please <u>complete</u> this application form.

   b. <u>Bring back</u> this application form.

   b. <u>Return</u> this application form.

   c. <u>Fill out</u> each card when you receive it.

   c. <u>Complete</u> each card when you receive it.

   d. <u>Mail back</u> each card.

   d. <u>Return</u> each card <u>by mail.</u>

   e. Where can I <u>find out</u> about special training for women?

   e. Where can I <u>get information</u> about special training for women?

   f. Well. Don't <u>give up</u>, Ana.

   f. Well. Don't <u>stop trying</u>, Ana.

   g. Can Tom <u>call</u> you <u>back</u>, Bill?

   g. Can Tom <u>return your telephone call</u>, Bill?

   h. I'm <u>thinking of</u> taking a course at night school.

   h. I'm <u>considering</u> taking a course at night school.

   i. I'm glad you could <u>drop in.</u>

   i. I'm glad you could <u>visit.</u>

5. Take a partner. One person reads a sentence from the right-hand column. The other person tries to remember the corresponding sentence from the left-hand column.

UNIT 28: APPLYING FOR A JOB

PHOTO STORY: Tony Gets A Job

10 Let me show you around. You can see what we do here.

11 We restore and sell pianos.

12 Many of them are very valuable.

13 Those pianos are very heavy. You need to be strong but you also need skill. We'll show you how to lift them.

14

15

16

17

DIALOGUES WITH CHOICES

See instructions on page 205.

I. Applying for a Job

A   1. Good morning. I saw your ad for (a piano mover). I'd like to apply.

    B   2. Oh yes. Have a seat.

A PIANO MOVER   A PAINTER   A CARPENTER   A WELDER

II. Asking for Permission

A   3. Do you mind if I (try this piano)?

    B   4. Go right ahead.
           5. No. Not at all. Go right ahead.
           6. Well, actually, I do mind.

TRY THIS PIANO   OPEN THE WINDOW   SIT HERE   SMOKE

PHOTOS WITHOUT WORDS

Look at the Photo Story on pages 228 to 232 and cover up the words in these photos: 1, 4, 7, 8, 16, 18, 19, 20.
Can you remember what the people are saying?

SPEAKING ACTIVITY WITH CHOICES

Take a partner. One of you is A. The other one is B. Follow the instructions below and make as many conversations as you can.

Applying for a Job

A is the applicant. B is the employer. B has put out an ad for a certain job that requires a class A licence.

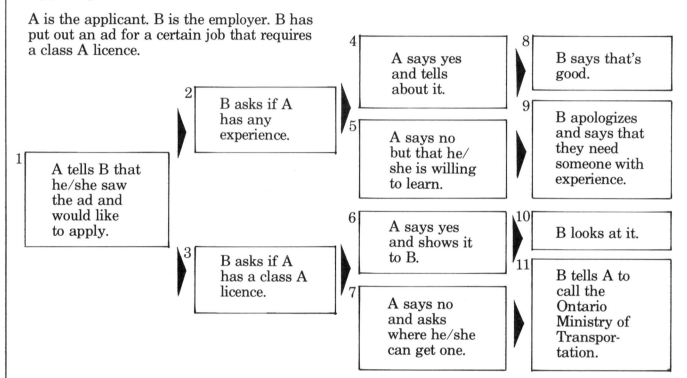

1 — A tells B that he/she saw the ad and would like to apply.

2 — B asks if A has any experience.

3 — B asks if A has a class A licence.

4 — A says yes and tells about it.

5 — A says no but that he/she is willing to learn.

6 — A says yes and shows it to B.

7 — A says no and asks where he/she can get one.

8 — B says that's good.

9 — B apologizes and says that they need someone with experience.

10 — B looks at it.

11 — B tells A to call the Ontario Ministry of Transportation.

PRONUNCIATION: Markings on Stressed Syllables

In the word **reference**, the first syllable gets the strongest stress. Different dictionaries use different markings to show this, for example:

1. 'ref er ence   2. ref'er ence   3. **ref** er ence

Look up these words in a dictionary and mark the syllable with the strongest stress. Use any markings you like.

a. advertisement   d. medical   g. understand

b. apply   e. valuable   h. certificate

c. licence   f. expect   i. beautiful

The answers are on page 272.

COMMUNICATION ACTIVITY: Job Interview

The class breaks up into groups of five, A, B, C, D and E. A and B are business partners in a restaurant. They have a job opening for a waiter or waitress. C, D and E are job applicants.

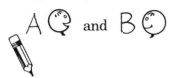   

1. Look in the box below.
   Decide together which duties you will want the new employee to perform.
   Put a check ✓ beside each.
   Decide together what abilities or knowledge you want your new employee to have.
   Put a check ✓ beside each.

In your notebook, write down the following information.
It can be fictitious.
— your experience
— your abilities and knowledge in restaurant work. (You can get a few ideas from the box below but don't write them all.)
— any questions you would like to ask the employer

Duties
— to wait on tables
— to help the cook occasionally
— to help mix alcoholic beverages at the bar
— to work split shift (for example, at lunch and dinner but not in the afternoon)

Abilities or Knowledge
— fluent English
— knowledge of food in general
— knowledge of the kind of food in this particular restaurant
   (for example — pizza, spaghetti, lasagna)
— fluency in the language of the country where the food originated
   (for example, French in a French-style restaurant)
— the ability to get along well with people

---

2. The employers, A and B together, interview each applicant in turn — first C, then D, then E.
   A and B ask about those items in the box that they have checked.

3. After the three interviews, A and B decide together which applicant is the best.

4. They tell the rest of the class why they made their particular choice.

Variations: You can do this activity again by substituting other jobs for waiter/waitress.

GRAMMAR: Two-word Verbs with Objects

1. Some two-word verbs take objects.

		TWO-WORD VERB	OBJECT
a.	He's	filling out	an application form.
b.	I'm	thinking of	taking a course.

2. An object can be a pronoun: **it**

3. Sentence a. has a separable two-word verb.
   You separate the verb from the particle to put the pronoun object between.

	VERB	PRONOUN OBJECT	PARTICLE
a.	He's	filling	it	out.

4. Sentence b. has an inseparable two-word verb.
   You put the pronoun object after it.

	TWO-WORD VERB	PRONOUN OBJECT
b.	I'm	thinking of	it.

5. Here are examples of two-word verbs with pronoun objects.
   The two-word verbs are underlined.

SEPARABLE
a. Here is the application form. Please <u>fill</u> it <u>out.</u>
b. Please <u>mail</u> it <u>back</u> right away.
c. Let me <u>show</u> you <u>around.</u>
d. Tom is not home now. Can he <u>call</u> you <u>back?</u>
e. Please complete this form and then <u>bring</u> it <u>back</u> to me.
f. Waiter, this cup is dirty. Please <u>take</u> it <u>back.</u>
g. Driver, I don't know where Queen Street is. Please <u>call</u> it <u>out.</u>

INSEPARABLE
h. I'm <u>thinking of</u> it.
i. Bring your children to my house. I'll <u>look after</u> them.
j. I didn't get my pay cheque. I asked my boss to <u>look into</u> it.
k. I <u>left</u> my house empty for three months. A thief <u>broke into</u> it.
l. I'll be in Paris at the same time as Ana. Maybe I'll <u>run into</u> her.

6. Write the numbers 1 to 10 in your notebook. Listen to the teacher say more sentences with two-word verbs. Is each two-word verb separable or inseparable? Write **S** or **I** beside each number.

CULTURAL DISCUSSION: Senior Citizens

Read this passage.

> Mr. Jenkins, Tony's employer, is 66 years old. People who are older than 65 are called senior citizens.
> Some people, Like Mr. Jenkins, continue to work. But some people stop working after 60 or 65.
> The government helps older people financially. Older people can also get special privileges like reduced prices at movies or free prescription drugs.
> Because people move around in their jobs, families get smaller and many older people live alone. However, there are social clubs and different interest groups that they can join.
> We usually call older people by their last names if we don't know them very well.

Listen to some statements. For each one, write **true** or **false** in your notebook.

Talk about older people in your native country.

USEFUL INFORMATION: Social Services for Seniors

Do you want information about financial help or special privileges for senior citizens? You can get this information from several places.

"Newcomers Guide to Services in Ontario" is a free booklet that comes in different languages. You can get it from the Ministry of Citizenship and Culture. Some libraries have it too. Read the section on "Social Services".

If you have a question, you can call the Seniors Secretariat at (416) 965-5106. They will answer collect telephone calls from any place in Ontario.

There is another booklet that you can read. It is called "Guide for Senior Citizens" and it comes in English or French. You can get it from the Seniors Secretariat.

Research:
Get a copy of "Newcomers Guide to Services in Ontario". Ask if it comes in your native language.

PHOTO STORY: Tony Gets His Medical

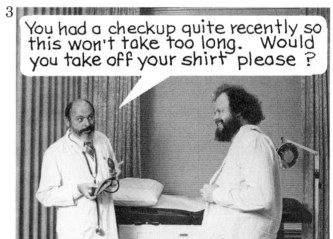

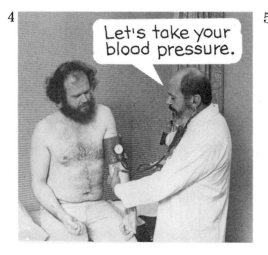

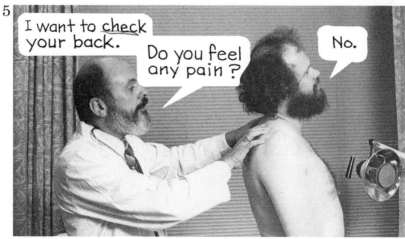

6

7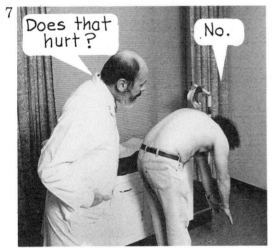

8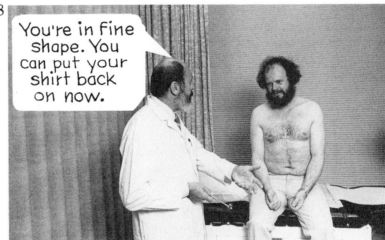

9

DIALOGUES WITH CHOICES

See instructions on page 205.

Physical Complaints

A   1. What's the problem?
    2. What's bothering you?

   B   3. My (back) hurts.
      4. I have pain in my (back).

BACK   SHOULDER   EYE   CHEST   STOMACH

A   5. How are you feeling?
    6. What's the problem?

   B   7. I have (a toothache).

A TOOTHACHE   AN EARACHE   A HEADACHE

A STOMACH-ACHE   A BACKACHE

A   8. What's bothering you?
    9. How are you feeling?

   B   10. I can't (breathe).
      11. It's hard for me to (breathe).

BREATHE   SEE AT A DISTANCE   SEE CLOSE UP

KEEP AWAKE   SLEEP AT NIGHT

A   12. What's the problem?
    13. What seems to be the problem? FORMAL

   B   14. I have trouble (breathing).
      15. I have difficulty (breathing).

BREATHING   SWALLOWING   WAKING

KEEPING AWAKE   SLEEPING AT NIGHT

LISTENING ACTIVITY: Doctor's Instructions

a. Before you begin, review the names of the parts of the body.
b. Listen to each instruction and follow it.

1. Hold out your arm.
2. Lift your arm.
3. Roll up your sleeve.
4. Breathe deeply.
5. Hold your breath. (Don't breathe.)
6. Breathe normally.
7. Turn around (Turn your back to me.)
8. Turn your head and look over your shoulder.

9. Put your chin on your chest.
10. Tilt your head back.
11. Bend to one side.
12. Bend to the other side.
13. Bend backwards.
14. Walk on your toes.
15. Make a fist.
16. Spread your fingers.

17. Open your mouth wide.
18. Stick out your tongue and say "aah".
19. Close your eyes.
20. Open your eyes.
21. Look up.
22. Look down.
23. Look to the right.
24. Look to the left.

Take a partner. One of you is A, the doctor. The other one is B, the patient. A gives doctors' instructions to B; B tries to follow them without looking at the pictures.

USEFUL INFORMATION: Medical Care

Keep your Ontario Health Insurance (OHIP) up to date by paying your premium every three months, <u>unless</u> your OHIP payments are made by your employer.

If you don't have enough money, ask if OHIP can help you pay your premiums. سیم

If you need to go into the hospital, OHIP pays for a bed in a <u>public ward</u>. OHIP does not pay for a <u>private</u> or <u>semi-private</u> room.

Some doctors <u>are in the</u> OHIP plan. You don't pay any money. The doctor sends your bill to OHIP, and OHIP pays the doctor.

Some doctors are not in the OHIP plan. You pay the doctor's bill yourself. You send the information to OHIP and OHIP sends you <u>back part</u> of the money.

پس دالیں بہ

When you go to a doctor for the first time, ask the <u>receptionist</u> if the doctor is in or out of OHIP.

Some <u>medical services</u> are not <u>covered</u> by OHIP, for example, <u>dental work</u> or glasses. سنڈار You can get private insurance for these services. قلب

There are other health services in Ontario. You can read about some of them in "Newcomers <u>Guide</u> to Services in Ontario".

You can also get information from the public health department in your city or <u>town. Look</u> ڈھونڈ in the blue pages of your telephone directory.

آبی

Research:
Find the telephone number of the public health department in your city or town. Write it down.

GRAMMAR: The Present Perfect Tense

1. In this sentence from photo no. 1, the verb **apply** is in the present perfect tense.

   Short form: I understand you've applied for a job.

   Long form: I understand you have applied for a job.

2. We can use the present perfect tense for an action that happened in the past when we are interested in the present result.

PRESENT PERFECT TENSE

a. You've applied for a job.
b. I've seen that movie.
c. We've been at the hospital all night.

PRESENT RESULT

Now you need a medical examination.
I don't want to see it again.
We're very tired now.

3. However, we sometimes use the past tense with present result, especially in informal speech.

Here are the same sentences in the past tense:

   a. You applied for a job. Now you need a medical examination.
   b. I saw that movie. I don't want to see it again.
   c. We were at the hospital all night. We're very tired now.

4. To make the present perfect tense, use **have** or **has** and the past participle.

SUBJECT	HAVE or HAS	PAST PARTICIPLE
I You We They	have or 've	applied for a job. seen that movie. been at the hospital all night. studied English before.
He She Tony	has or 's	done this kind of work before. waited for my friend for an hour. called the fire department.

Practice saying some of the sentences in the box.

5. With regular verbs, the past participle is the same as the past tense form: **applied, studied, waited, called.**

Complete each sentence below. Use the present perfect tense.

   a. We ___ _____ Paris many times. We don't want to visit there this year.

   b. I ___ _____ English before; I don't want to go into class 1.

   c. She ___ _____ an ambulance. It will be here very soon.

   d. He ___ _____ for three years without a holiday. He's very tired.

6. With irregular verbs, the past participle is sometimes different from the past tense form.

PAST PARTICIPLE	seen	been	done
PAST TENSE FORM	saw	was, were	did

Complete each sentence below. Use the present perfect tense.
If you don't know the past participle, look on pages 273 - 274.

   e. I ___ _____ my wallet; I'm very worried.
   f. Mary ___ _____ this movie; she doesn't want to see it again.
   g. I ___ _____ this book. I think you'll like it.
   h. The teacher ___ _____ this lesson before. I remember it.

The answers for 5. and 6. are on page 272.

READING AND WRITING: Confidential Health History

Fill this form out for a cousin or other relative.

HEALTH HISTORY

Past Illnesses (including Childhood Illnesses, High Blood Pressure, Heart Disease, Diabetes, Thyroid Disease, Cancer)

Operations	Allergies
Accidents	Immunization
Hospitalizations	Medications (Prescription - other)

T. B. Skin Test ☐ Yes ☐ No	Date of Last Test	Result	Chest X-Ray ☐ Yes ☐ No	Date of Last One	Reason

Do you now or have you ever suffered from any of the following? Check (✔) if the answer is yes.

Recent Change in Weight _____ ☐
Recent Fatigue or Weakness _____ ☐
Head Injury or Concussion _____ ☐
Fainting Spells or Dizziness _____ ☐
Frequent Headaches _____ ☐
Epilepsy or Convulsions _____ ☐
Ear Aches or Ear Infections _____ ☐
Ear Noises or Deafness _____ ☐
Eye Irritation or Infection _____ ☐
Vision Problems _____ ☐
Nose or Throat Problems _____ ☐
Sinus Trouble _____ ☐
Frequent Colds / Sore Throats _____ ☐
Tooth or Gum Trouble _____ ☐
Skin Rashes, Itchiness, Burning _____ ☐
Hives, Hay Fever, Asthma _____ ☐
Allergy to Drugs _____ ☐
Anemia, Blood Conditions _____ ☐
Chronic Cough _____ ☐

Lung Disease, i.e. T.B., Pneumonia, Bronchitis, Emphysema _____ ☐
Shortness of Breath _____ ☐
Heart Trouble _____ ☐
Chest Pain, Pressure, Tightness _____ ☐
Ulcers, Stomach Trouble _____ ☐
Indigestion, Nausea, Vomiting _____ ☐
Abdominal Pain _____ ☐
Bowel Trouble _____ ☐
Kidney or Bladder Trouble _____ ☐
Neck or Back Injury or Pain _____ ☐
Low Back Pain _____ ☐
Rheumatism or Arthritis _____ ☐
Breast Problems, Lumps _____ ☐
Foot Problems _____ ☐
Problems Sleeping _____ ☐
Have you any restriction on physical activity? _____ ☐
Other _____ ☐

UNIT 30: GETTING A MISTAKE CORRECTED

PHOTO STORY: Ana's Pay Cheque is Wrong

246

DIALOGUES WITH CHOICES

See instructions on page 205.

I. Complaining About An Error

A 1. Excuse me. I think there's a mistake on my (pay cheque).
2. Excuse me. I think there's an error on my (pay cheque).
3. Excuse me. I think someone made a mistake on my (pay cheque).

B 4. Oh? What's the problem?
5. Oh? What is it?

PAY CHEQUE   ATTENDANCE REPORT   BILL

II. Specifying the Error

A 6. I worked three hours overtime (last week). I didn't get paid for it.

B 7. Okay. Leave it with me. I'll look into it.
8. Okay. Leave it with me. I'll check into it.

LAST WEEK   MONDAY NIGHT   ON SATURDAY

III. Following Up on a Complaint

A 9. Did you get a chance to ask about my (overtime)?
10. Did you have a chance to ask about my (overtime)?

B 11. Oh yes. Don't worry. You'll get it in your next pay cheque.

OVERTIME   VACATION PAY   SICK PAY

PHOTOS WITHOUT WORDS

Look at the Photo Story on pages 245 and 246 and cover up the words in these photos: 1, 2
3, 4, 5, 9.
Can you remember what the people are saying?

SPEAKING ACTIVITY WITH CHOICES

Take a partner. One of you is A. The other one is B. Follow the instructions below and make as many conversations as you can.

Wondering What to Do

A and B are workers. A has just received a pay cheque with a mistake on it.

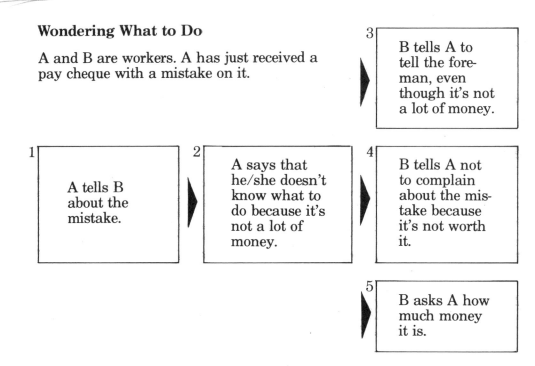

1 A tells B about the mistake.

2 A says that he/she doesn't know what to do because it's not a lot of money.

3 B tells A to tell the foreman, even though it's not a lot of money.

4 B tells A not to complain about the mistake because it's not worth it.

5 B asks A how much money it is.

READING: Statement of Earnings

When Ana got her pay cheque, she got this statement of earnings with it.

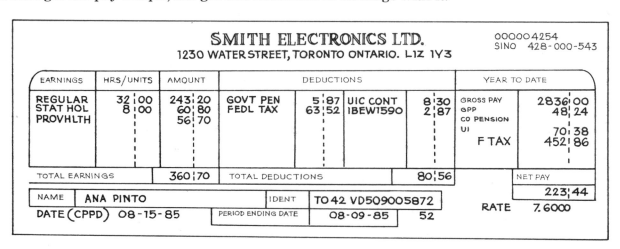

								YEAR TO DATE	
EARNINGS	HRS/UNITS	AMOUNT	DEDUCTIONS						
REGULAR	32:00	243:20	GOVT PEN	5:87	UIC CONT	8:30	GROSS PAY		2836:00
STAT HOL	8:00	60:80	FEDL TAX	63:52	IBEW1590	2:87	GPP		48:24
PROVHLTH		56:70					CO PENSION		
							UI		70:38
							F TAX		452:86
TOTAL EARNINGS		360:70	TOTAL DEDUCTIONS			80:56	NET PAY		223:44

SMITH ELECTRONICS LTD.
1230 WATER STREET, TORONTO ONTARIO. L1Z 1Y3
000004254 SINO 428-000-543

NAME ANA PINTO   IDENT TO42 VD509005872
DATE (CPPD) 08-15-85   PERIOD ENDING DATE 08-09-85   52
RATE 7.6000

Note: To arrive at $223.44 (NET PAY), subtract $80.56 (TOTAL DEDUCTIONS) from $304.00 (TOTAL EARNINGS excluding PROV. HEALTH premium).

Here are some short forms from the statement of earnings on page 248. Match the long form to the short form and put the letter in the box.

1 [B] HRS ←

2 [A] STAT HOL

3 [F] PROVHLTH

4 [E] GOVT PEN or GPP
   or CPP

5 [H] FEDL TAX or FTAX

6 [D] UIC CONT or UI

7 [G] IBEW

8 [G] CO PENSION

9 [ ] RATE

A. Statutory holiday(s)

B. Hours (number of hours worked)

C. International Brotherhood of
   Electrical Workers (union)

D. Unemployment Insurance Commission
   contributions

E. Government Pension Plan (Canada
   Pension Plan)

F. Provincial Health Plan (OHIP)

G. Company Pension Plan

H. Federal Tax

I. Rate of pay per hour

Look at Ana's statement of earnings on page 248 and answer these questions in your notebook.

1. How many hours did Ana work this week?
2. How many hours did she get paid for?
3. How much money did she earn for these 40 hours?
4. What are Ana's total earnings according to this statement?
5. Why is there a difference between these last two figures?
6. How much money did the company deduct for union dues?
7. How much money did the company deduct this time for the Canada Pension Plan?
8. How much money has the company deducted for the Canada Pension Plan all year until now?
9. How much federal tax did the company deduct this time?
10. How much federal tax has the company deducted all year until now?
11. How much money did Ana earn this time after all the deductions?
12. How much money does Ana earn per hour?

The answers are on page 272.

USEFUL INFORMATION: Employment Standards

Most workers in Ontario are protected by the Employment Standards Act. This law gives you certain rights as a worker.

For example, it sets the minimum wage, that is, the minimum hourly rates of pay. It sets the maximum number of hours that you can work per day and week, and a rate for overtime pay.

It sets the number of paid public holidays, and the minimum amount of vacation pay that you get.

If you are expecting a baby, you are entitled to a minimum number of weeks of pregnancy leave without pay, and the employer must take you back. You may be eligible for unemployment insurance benefits during this period.

According to the Employment Standards Act, a man and a woman must get equal pay for equal work.

If you have a problem, ask your union to help you, or go to the Employment Standards Branch of the Ministry of Labour.

For detailed information, read items 1, 2 or 3 below. They come in different languages, and they are free.
1. "Newcomers Guide to Services in Ontario". Telephone the Ontario Ministry of Citizenship and Culture.
2. "A Guide to the Employment Standards Act". Telephone the Ontario Ministry of Labour.
3. Pamphlets about workers' rights. Telephone the Ontario Women's Directorate.

You can find all three telephone numbers in your telephone directory. Look in the blue pages.

Research:
Do you have a specific question about employment standards? Try to find the answer and bring it to class.

GRAMMAR: Negative Statements in the Present Perfect

1. Here is a sentence from photo no. 3 in the photo story.
   Short form: They haven't paid me my overtime.
   Long form: They have not paid me my overtime.
2. To make a negative sentence in the present perfect tense, take the affirmative and add **not** or **n't** after the auxiliary **have** or **has**.

AFFIRMATIVE:	He has applied for a job.	We have done this kind of work before.
NEGATIVE:	He has not applied for a job.	We have not done this kind of work before.
	He hasn't applied for a job.	We haven't done this kind of work before.

3. L k at the affirmative sentences in number 4 on page 243. Make as many negative nces as you can.

UNIT 31: LOOKING FOR A ROOM

PHOTO STORY: Ana Has to Move

9

10

11

12

DIALOGUES WITH CHOICES

See instructions on page 205.

I. Telling What You're Doing

A 1. I've been busy. I'm looking for (another place).

B 2. Good luck. I hope you find something good.

ANOTHER PLACE A JOB A NURSERY FOR MY CHILD A HOUSE

II. Inviting Someone to Join You

A 3. I'm going (to look at a room). Do you feel like coming along?

B 4. Sure.
   5. Not right now. Thanks.

TO LOOK AT A ROOM TO SEE A MOVIE

TO VISIT SOME FRIENDS TO TAKE A WALK

III. Asking to See Something

A 6. Can I see (the washroom)?
   7. Could I see (the washroom)?
   8. I'd like to see (the washroom).

B 9. Of course. It's just down the hall.
   10. Of course. It's right this way.

A 11. How many people share (the washroom)?

B 12. Just three. You and two other tenants.

THE WASHROOM THE LAUNDRY ROOM THE KITCHEN

PHOTOS WITHOUT WORDS

Look at the Photo Story on pages 251 to 253 and cover up the words. Can you remember what the people are saying?

SPEAKING ACTIVITY WITH CHOICES

Take a partner. One of you is A. The other one is B. Follow each set of instructions below and make as many conversations as you can.

I. Talking About a Room

A and B are neighbours.
A has just looked at a room and is talking to B.

1 A says that he/she has just looked at a room.

2 B asks if A likes it.

3 A says yes and that he/she is going to take it.

4 A says no and that he/she will keep looking.

5 A says that he/she isn't sure and gives a reason.

6 B says that he/she is glad that A found something.

7 B offers to help.

Example for no. 5:
I'm not sure. It's a bit small. I don't know if it's worth the money.

Examples for no. 7:
a. I can come and look at the room if you like.
b. Would you like me to come and look at the room?

II. Getting Information About a Room

A is looking at a room.
B is the landlord or landlady.

8 A asks about a lease.

9 B responds.

10 A asks about laundry facilities.

11 B responds.

Example for no. 8:
Is there a lease?

Examples for no. 10:
a. Are there laundry facilities?
b. Do you have laundry facilities?

A continues asking B more questions about the room.

255

GRAMMAR I: Would like

1. In this sentence from photo no. 7, Ana is telling what she wants, in a polite way.

    Short form: I'd like to think about it.

    Long form: I would like to think about it.

2. **Would like** is the same for all persons.

I You He She We They	would like 'd like	to think about it. to see the washroom. to find a better room. to find a place nearby. a better room. a place nearby.

    Look in the box above and make as many sentences as you can.

3. a. Make personal sentences about yourself telling what you would like.

    b. Make sentences about relatives or friends, telling what they would like.

4. To make a question, put the subject between **Would** and **like**.

SUBJECT

Would	you	like	to think about it?

5. Here are some offers with **Would like:**

    Would you like some coffee?
    Would you like another piece of cake?

6. Here is an invitation:

    Would you like to come for dinner at our place on Saturday?
    <u>or</u>
    Can you come for dinner at our place on Saturday? INFORMAL

7. The sentence below can be a suggestion, or an invitation — that is, at the speaker's expense.
    In what situations do you think it is a suggestion, and in what situations do you think it is an invitation?

    Would you like to see a movie?

COMMUNICATION ACTIVITY: Locations in a Room

Listen to each location. Look at the room below; what is the corresponding number?

a. against the wall under the clock
b. in the centre of the room
c. next to the window
d. against the wall next to the picture
e. against the wall under the picture
f. in the corner between the window and the picture
g. against the wall to the left of the door
h. against the wall to the right of the door
 i. in the corner next to the window

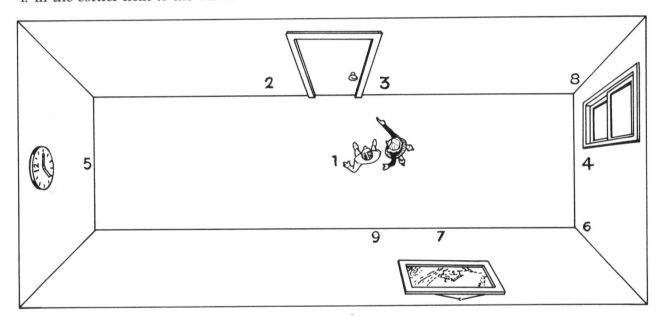

a. Tear out each picture card at the bottom of the page.
b. Take a partner.
c. Put one picture card on each number in the room. Your partner doesn't look.
d. Your partner takes each picture card from his/her pile and says:
   Where does the (couch) go?
e. You give instructions according to where your own (couch) is placed.
f. When all your partner's picture cards are placed, check to make sure both rooms look the same.

couch or sofa	armchair	lamp	piano	coffee table	side or end table	rocking chair	rug or carpet	stereo system

       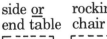

USEFUL INFORMATION: The Ontario Human Rights Code

Suppose that you want to rent a certain room or apartment.

The landlord or landlady says "no" because of your accent, or where you come from, or the colour of your skin.

These are not valid reasons. This is called discrimination. The Ontario Human Rights Code protects you against different kinds of discrimination.

According to this Code, no one can refuse you a certain job or place to live because of your sex, skin colour, race, age, religion or handicap.

There are more forms of discrimination. You can read about them in a pamphlet called "Human Rights in Ontario". You can get this in different languages from the Ontario Human Rights Commission.

In some cases the Human Rights Code does not apply. One case is where the tenant shares a bathroom or kitchen with the landlord or landlady, or his or her family.

If you have a complaint about discrimination, or if you want more information, contact the nearest office of the Ontario Human Rights Commission, Ministry of Labour.

Research:
Find the telephone number of the Ontario Human Rights Commission. Look in the white pages or blue pages of your telephone directory. Bring the number to class.

USEFUL INFORMATION: Changing Your Address

Suppose that you are moving to a new address and you want to make sure that all your mail goes to your new address.

First go to the post office and get some "Change of Address Announcements". Mail these cards to your friends, relatives and business associates.

Then make sure that no other mail goes to your old address. Ask the post office to redirect your mail to your new address. You fill out a form called, "Request for Redirection of Mail". This service is for a specific period of time, and you pay a small charge.

Suppose that you don't want your mail to go to your new address. Ask the post office to hold your mail so that you can pick it up yourself. You fill out a "Request for Holding of Mail". Again, this service is for a specific period of time and there is a small charge.

stereo system	rug or carpet	rocking chair	side or end table	coffee table	piano	lamp	armchair	couch or sofa

GRAMMAR II: Reflexive Pronouns

1. The sentence below, from photo no. 1, contains the reflexive pronoun **myself**. **Myself** reflects back to the subject **I**. The sentence means **I am in the house alone.** No other person is in the house.

   I've got the house to myself.

2. Here are some reflexive pronouns, and words that they reflect back to.

   Singular
   I .a.m. in. the. ho.. myself
   you .... yourself
   he .... himself
   she .... herself

   Plural
   we .... ourselves
   you .... yourselves
   they .... themselves

3. Complete each sentence below with a reflexive pronoun.

   a. Jean's got the house to _herself_ .

   b. We've got the cafeteria to _ourselves_

   c. I'd like to have the house to _myself_

   d. They had the whole beach to _themselves_

4. The reflexive pronoun has many different uses. Here is another example. In the sentence below, **by herself** means **alone**, that is with no other person. **Herself** reflects back to the subject Ana.
   Ana lives in a room by herself.

5. Complete each sentence below with a reflexive pronoun.

   e. I looked for a room by _myself_ ; no one went with me.

   f. Ana didn't look for a room by _herself_; her neighbour Jean went with her.

   g. I went to the movies by _myself_ ; no one went with me.

   h. Bob didn't go to the movies by _himself_; he took the kids with him.

6. Sometimes we use the reflexive pronoun for emphasis. In the sentence below, from page 258, the reflexive pronoun **yourself** reflects back to the subject **you**. It emphasizes that **you** pick it (the mail) up. The mail carrier does not pick it up, and no other person picks it up.
   Ask the post office to hold your mail so that you can pick it up yourself.

7. Complete this sentence with a reflexive pronoun.

   i. Some doctors are not in the OHIP plan; you pay the doctor's bill _yourself_

The answers are on page 272.

PHOTO STORY: The McMichael Canadian Collection

14

15

16

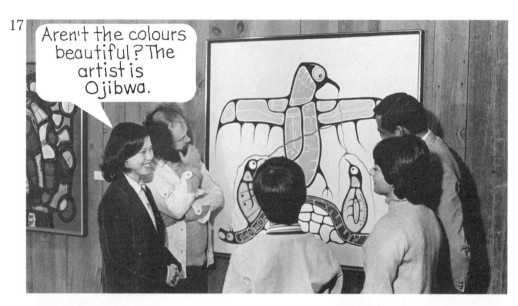

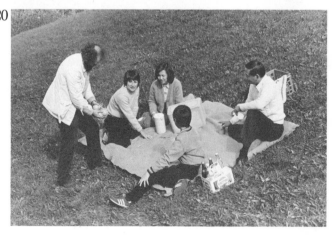

DIALOGUES WITH CHOICES

See instructions on page 205.

I. Suggestions

A 1. Let's go to (the McMichael Collection).
   2. Why don't we go to (the McMichael Collection)?

   B 3. Okay. Good idea. INFORMAL
      4. Yes. That's a good idea.

THE McMICHAEL COLLECTION   A MOVIE   A CONCERT   THE MUSEUM

II. Suggestions

A 5. (Ana's) been there. Maybe (she)'d like to come with us.

   B 6. Why don't you give (her) a call?
      7. I'll give (her) a call.

ANA   TONY   LOU   SU PING

III. Prohibitions

A 8. You can't drink that (in the park). It's against the law.

   B 9. Okay. I'll leave it at your place and we'll drink it when we get back.

IN THE PARK   ON THE STREET   ON THE SUBWAY   IN THE CAR

PHOTOS WITHOUT WORDS

Look at the Photo Story on pages 260 to 264 and cover up the words in these photos:
1-3, 5-9, 12-18.
Can you remember what the people are saying?

SPEAKING ACTIVITY WITH CHOICES

Take a partner. One of you is A. The other one is B. Follow the instructions below and make as many conversations as you can.

Offering to Treat Someone

A and B are in a restaurant together. They have finished eating and the waiter has brought the bill.

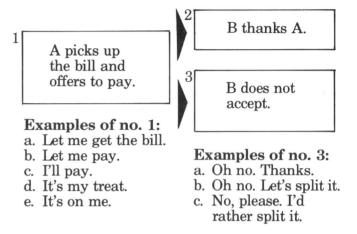

1 | A picks up the bill and offers to pay.

2 | B thanks A.

3 | B does not accept.

Examples of no. 1:
a. Let me get the bill.
b. Let me pay.
c. I'll pay.
d. It's my treat.
e. It's on me.

Examples of no. 3:
a. Oh no. Thanks.
b. Oh no. Let's split it.
c. No, please. I'd rather split it.

LISTENING ACTIVITY: Bus Schedule

When you call for information about bus schedules, you can say, **When does the bus go to (Kleinburg)?**
Here are some typical answers for short-trip buses:

1. every hour on the hour
2. 25 minutes to each hour
3. five after and 35 after each hour
4. every hour on the half hour
5. on a 20-minute service: on the hour, twenty past and twenty to
6. on a 30-minute service: at a quarter past and a quarter to the hour.

Below are parts of the corresponding bus schedules. Listen to the teacher say an answer from above. Which schedule below corresponds? Give the letter.

A.	7:30	8:30	9:30	10:30	D.	7:00	7:20	7:40	8:00
B.	7:15	7:45	8:15	8:45	E.	7:05	7:35	8:05	8:35
C.	7:00	8:00	9:00	10:00	F.	7:35	8:35	9:35	10:35

The answers are on page 272.

READING AND WRITING: Entertainment

Look in the Entertainment section of the newspaper. Find some things that look interesting to you (or your child), for example: a movie, play, concert or museum exhibit. If the location, time and cost are good for you, write the information in the box below.

A ENTERTAINMENT ITEM	B LOCATION	C OF INTEREST TO…	D DATES	E TIMES	F COST
1.					
2.					
3.					

Find someone else in your class who is interested in the same thing(s) that you are. For a speaking activity, make plans to go together.

USEFUL INFORMATION: You and the Law

In the photo story Lou told Tony that it's against the law to drink liquor in the park. If you have questions about the law, there are several places where you can get answers.

You can read about some of these places in "Newcomers Guide to Services in Ontario". It has a section entitled "The Law in Ontario".

This section also tells you how to find a lawyer, and where to get legal aid if you can't afford to pay a lawyer.

You can also go to an immigrant aid agency, library or community information centre. They will give you information or refer you to other places.

Research:
Do you have any questions about the law? One way that you can get answers is by calling the "Dial a Law" telephone number.
Follow these instructions:
1. Write down one question in your notebook.
2. Look in the Yellow Pages telephone directory under "Lawyers".
3. Write down the "Dial a Law" telephone number.
4. Call the number and ask your question.
5. If you don't understand the answer, ask a native speaker of English to call and ask the question again, and to tell you the answer.
6. Write down the answer.
7. Read your question and answer to the class.

For sources of more information about life in Ontario, see page 269.

READING: Ontario's Major Industries

Mining
About eighty percent of Ontario is very rocky. We mine nickel, copper, gold, silver, iron, uranium, zinc and other minerals in the North.

Forestry
There are many forests in Northern Ontario. From the trees we get pulp and paper.

Manufacturing
Southern Ontario is the manufacturing centre of Canada. Ontario exports motor cars and parts, steel products, chemicals, newsprint, aircraft, and office machines, among other things.

Farming
Southern Ontario is a very productive farming area. We get meat and poultry, and dairy products like milk and eggs, from Ontario farms. The Niagara Peninsula is rich in fruit, for example: grapes, apples, peaches, pears and berries.

Hydro-electric Power
Ontario's many rivers provide us with power. We also get power from the famous Niagara Falls.

Draw these symbols on the map to show the location of Ontario's major industries.

USEFUL INFORMATION: Where to Find It

In this course we have given you some "Useful Information" about life in Ontario. If you want more information, there are many places where you can find it.

Immigrant Aid Agencies
They may have someone who speaks your native language. If you have a problem, they will try to help you or refer you to another place. Look in the white pages of your telephone directory. Look under the name of your nationality, for example "Italian" or "Vietnamese".

Citizens' Inquiry
They have information about services, especially government services. However, if you ask them some other kind of question, they will try to find you the answer. You can write a letter in your native language to: Ontario 20, Queen's Park, Toronto. Or you can telephone collect from anywhere in Ontario to (416) 965-3535.

"Newcomers Guide to Services in Ontario"
This booklet is free of charge and comes in different languages. It is published by the Ontario Ministry of Citizenship and Culture. You can also get it at some libraries, community centres or immigrant aid agencies.

Community Information Centres
Most centres are listed in the Appendix of "Newcomers Guide to Services in Ontario". You can also look in the white pages of your telephone directory under "Information".

Libraries
Look in the white pages of your telephone directory under "Public Libraries".

Government Services
Look in the blue pages of your telephone directory.

Research:
Find a community information centre or immigrant aid agency that is near your home. Write down the name, address and telephone number.

Telephoning for Information: Some Tips

Let's say that you have a telephone number, but not the name of a person.

When you call you can say "I'd like some information about…" You may have to repeat this more than once. It can take several calls before you get the right person.

When you get the right person, it's a good idea to say: "May I please have your name in case we get cut off?"

Page 136

2. nervous   3. fine   4. happy
5. angry/upset   6. sick
7. tired   8. hot   9. cold

Page 140

3c. I'm tired.
 d. They're from Chile.
 e. We're musicians.
 f. They're angry.
 g. We're from China.
 h. We're happy.

Page 141

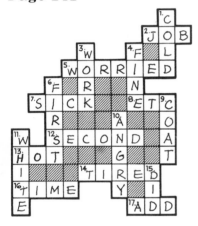

Page 148

3b. I'll call the doctor.
 c. I'll call the Emergency/the hospital.
 d. I'll get another pencil.
 e. I'll get another seat/chair.
 f. I'll call the plumber.
 g. I'll get coffee.
 h. I'll get stamps.

Page 149

4b. He wants to live in Ottawa.
 c. She wants to play the piano.
 d. I want to eat lunch.
 f. He doesn't want to take the bus.
 g. I don't want to work.
 h. They don't want to take the bus.

Page 153

5b. He didn't eat.
 c. He didn't watch television.
 d. He didn't play the piano.
 e. He didn't play the clarinet.
 f. He didn't walk.
 g. He didn't visit friends.
 h. He didn't call the hospital.

Page 157

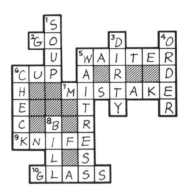

Page 159

B.1   C.3   D.2   E.3   F.2

Page 163

 c. She can touch her toes.
 d. We can't watch television on Thursday.
 e. I can watch television on Friday.
 f. I can't touch my toes.
 g. We can't visit friends on Tuesday.
 h. They can work on Saturday.

Page 170

4b. I'm not from China.
  c. She's not a waitress.
  d. They're not nervous/afraid/etc.
  e. We're not from Portugal.
  f. We're not painters.
  g. He's not sick.
  h. She's not happy.

Pages 174-175

	2a. ✗	3a. ✓
	b. ✗	b. ✗
4a. ✗	5a. ✓	6a. ✗
		b. ✓
7a. ✗	8a. ✓	9a. ✗
	b. ✗	b. ✗
10a. ✗	11a. ✗	12a. ✗
b. ✓	b. ✓	
13a. ✓	14a. ✓	15a. ✗
b. ✗		b. ✓
c. ✗		

Page 176

3c. When will my car be ready?
  How much will it cost?
  d. When will my watch be ready?
  How much will it cost?
  e. When will my boots be ready?
  How much will they cost?
  f. When will my coat be <u>ready?</u> آیا کارد و
  How much will it cost?

Page 183

a. English, French, History, Science, Family
  Studies, Art
b. Math
c. French, History
d. Art
e. Music
f. Math

Page 184

  c. She does the laundry on Saturdays.
  d. We do the shopping on Friday evenings.
  e. He does his homework at eight o'clock.
  f. They do the shopping on Mondays.
  g. He does the dishes at seven-thirty.
  h. I do the <u>laundry</u> on Thursdays.

Page 193

3c. This is her first job.
  d. This is your pencil.
  e. This is his hat.
  f. This is our house.
  g. This is her coffee.
  h. This is their baby.
  i. This is her glove.

Page 194

1. b   2. b   3. a

Page 200

4b. She's eating.
  c. She's reading.
  d. They're watching television.
6f. I'm visiting friends on Thursday.
  g. We're watching television at nine o'clock.
  h. They're moving on Saturday.

Page 201

2. an 'oth er
3. 'show er
4. ex 'pect ing
5. 'some thing
6. 'bet ter
7. de 'li cious
8. 'wel come
9. 'sup per

Page 209

1. a Canada Employment Centre
2. the Apprenticeship Branch of the Ministry of Colleges and Universities
3a. A Canada Employment Centre is one of the places where you can go.
 b. Ask an employer if she/he can train you.
4. Ontario Ministry of Education correspondence courses

Page 218

1. yes
2. on any days
3. during any hours
4. piano or clarinet: teaching or playing
5. house painting, furniture moving
6. $16.00 an hour
7. close to Toronto

Page 219

2b. I won't find what I want on the job boards.
 c. Tony won't get a job.
 d. It won't take ten minutes to fill this prescription.
 e. The bus won't arrive at seven-thirty.

Page 220

2. to mor' row
3. in sur' ance
4. com plete'
5. paint' er
6. as sist' ant
7. yes' ter day
8. noth' ing
9. mu si' cian
10. in' ter est ed
11. cer' tain ly

Page 226

2.D   3.A   4.F   5.B   6.G   7.E
8.I   9.J   10.H

Page 234

a. ad ver' tise ment
b. ap ply'
c. li' cence
d. med' i cal
e. val' u a ble
f. ex pect'
g. un der stand'
h. cer tif' i cate
i. beau' ti ful

Page 243

5a. We've visited Paris many times.
 b. I've studied English before;
 c. She's called an ambulance.
 d. He's worked for three years without a holiday.
6e. I've lost my wallet;
 f. Mary has seen this movie;
 g. I've read this book.
 h. The teacher has taught this lesson before.

Page 249

2.A   3.F   4.E   5.H   6.D   7.C
8.G   9.I

1. 32 hours
2. 40 hours (including Statutory holidays)
3. $304.00
4. $360.70
5. The larger figure includes PROVHLTH (OHIP premium), which the company pays.
6. $ 2.87
7. $ 5.87
8. $ 48.24
9. $ 63.52
10. $452.86
11. $223.44 (net pay)
12. $ 7.60

Page 259

3b. ourselves
 c. myself
 d. themselves
5f. herself
 g. myself
 h. himself
7i. yourself

Page 266

1.C   2.F   3.E   4.A   5.D   6.B

APPENDIX

IRREGULAR VERBS

SIMPLE FORM	PRESENT PARTICIPLE	PAST FORM	PAST PARTICIPLE
be	being	was, were	been
become	becoming	became	become
begin	beginning	began	begun
bite	biting	bit	bitten
blow	blowing	blew	blown
break	breaking	broke	broken
bring	bringing	brought	brought
build	building	built	built
burn	burning	burnt (burned)	burnt (burned)
buy	buying	bought	bought
catch	catching	caught	caught
choose	choosing	chose	chosen
come	coming	came	come
cost	costing	cost	cost
cut	cutting	cut	cut
do	doing	did	done
draw	drawing	drew	drawn
dream	dreaming	dreamt (dreamed)	dreamt (dreamed)
drink	drinking	drank	drunk
drive	driving	drove	driven
eat	eating	ate	eaten
fall	falling	fell	fallen
feel	feeling	felt	felt
fight	fighting	fought	fought
find	finding	found	found
fly	flying	flew	flown
forget	forgetting	forgot	forgotten
get	getting	got	got (gotten)
give	giving	gave	given
go	going	went	gone
grow	growing	grew	grown
hang	hanging	hung	hung
have	having	had	had
hear	hearing	heard	heard
hide	hiding	hid	hidden
hit	hitting	hit	hit
hold	holding	held	held
hurt	hurting	hurt	hurt
keep	keeping	kept	kept
know	knowing	knew	known
lead	leading	led	led
learn	learning	learnt (learned)	learnt (learned)
leave	leaving	left	left

273

SIMPLE FORM	PRESENT PARTICIPLE	PAST FORM	PAST PARTICIPLE
lend	lending	lent	lent
let	letting	let	let
lie	lying	lay	lain
lose	losing	lost	lost
make	making	made	made
mean	meaning	meant	meant
meet	meeting	met	met
put	putting	put	put
read	reading	read	read
rid	ridding	rid	rid
ride	riding	rode	ridden
run	running	ran	run
say	saying	said	said
see	seeing	saw	seen
sell	selling	sold	sold
send	sending	sent	sent
set	setting	set	set
shoot	shooting	shot	shot
show	showing	showed	showed (shown)
sing	singing	sang	sung
sit	sitting	sat	sat
sleep	sleeping	slept	slept
smell	smelling	smelt (smelled)	smelt (smelled)
speak	speaking	spoke	spoken
spend	spending	spent	spent
spread	spreading	spread	spread
stand	standing	stood	stood
steal	stealing	stole	stolen
stick	sticking	stuck	stuck
swim	swimming	swam	swum
take	taking	took	taken
teach	teaching	taught	taught
tear	tearing	tore	torn
tell	telling	told	told
think	thinking	thought	thought
throw	throwing	threw	thrown
try	trying	tried	tried
understand	understanding	understood	understood
wake	waking	woke	woken
wear	wearing	wore	worn
win	winning	won	won
write	writing	wrote	written

I don't care

social insurance
driver's licence.
medical insurance
unemployment insurance
S.I.N health insurance